growing the NORTHEAST garden

growing the NORTHEAST garden

ANDREW KEYS
Photography by KERRY MICHAELS

Timber Press
Portland • London

Frontispiece: A well-designed landscape ignites the senses. This moment appears in the garden of Gordon and Mary Hayward, Putney, Vermont.

Published in 2015 by Timber Press, Inc.
Photo credits appear on page 293.

The Haseltine Building
133 S.W. Second Avenue, Suite 450
Portland, Oregon 97204-3527
timberpress.com

6a Lonsdale Road
London NW6 6RD
timberpress.co.uk

Printed in China
Book design by Jane Jeszeck

Library of Congress Cataloging-in-Publication Data
Keys, Andrew.
Growing the Northeast garden/Andrew Keys; photography by Kerry Michaels.—First edition.
pages cm
Includes bibliographical references and index.
ISBN 978-1-60469-448-2 — ISBN 978-1-60469-496-3 1. Gardening—Northeastern States.
2. Plants,
Ornamental—Northeastern States. I. Michaels, Kerry. II. Title.
SB453.2.N82K49 2014
635.0974—dc23
2014010461

A catalog record for this book is also available from the British Library.

For BK—AK

For Brett, Ethan, and Maya—KM

Contents

PREFACE

HELLO! As the writer and photographer of *Growing the Northeast Garden*, we would like to take a moment to personally say thank you for picking up this book. If you haven't skipped ahead to the photos of beautiful plants, you may be wondering who we are. Here's a brief synopsis of our paths as gardeners and authors.

Though he's called Massachusetts home since 2001, Andrew hails from the South, and remembers long summer days playing barefoot in the woods. It was there he first discovered plants, and a lifelong love affair was born. When he grew up and moved north, Andrew endeavored to learn absolutely everything about gardening in the Northeast. Fortunately, he believes learning is the most rewarding aspect of planting a garden—experiments abound in his own yard north of Boston. The narrative of this book reflects Andrew's passion for helping others discover such rewards, and he feels privileged to have the opportunity to share what he's learned with you.

Kerry, on the other hand, is a lifelong resident of the Northeast: Connecticut, Vermont, New Hampshire, Massachusetts, and New York City. Like Andrew, Kerry was raised with a love for the outdoors. She has worked on farms, though she now focuses on small gardens and containers. She discovered the Northeast as a gardener in 2001, when she moved from Manhattan to her home on the coast of Maine. Kerry feels that gardening has changed her, quieted her, and that photographing plants and gardens has transformed the way she sees the world. The beautiful imagery shared in this book is largely courtesy of Kerry's talented eye.

In case you hadn't gathered from getting to know us, we are real gardeners. Sure, we know a thing or two, but Mother Nature is a great equalizer, and the playing field that is the garden is much more level than you might imagine. Consider this book a compendium of lessons we've learned in our time as Northeast gardeners, but know that we and everyone who's decided to plant and grow living things is learning something new all the time. (And don't let anyone tell you otherwise!) Even if you're just beginning to learn, you're always in good company.

In this book, we've attempted to present plants and gardens that, while they may be gorgeous and inspiring, also have practical value. Maybe you're dubious as to your ability to grow a garden as beautiful as those in the Design section (you shouldn't be), but perhaps a small corner of one of those gardens will call out to you and say, "Yes! This is something you can do in *your* yard!" Guess what? That is how all beautiful gardens begin.

Writing and photographing this book has been a joy for us, so it's been easy to focus on the most important lesson of all: gardening, above all, should be fun. Humans grow plants for food, clothing, and shelter, but this book is about building a landscape to beautify your world. This type of landscape, first and foremost, should bring you joy. Build your garden with joy in mind, and we believe you're guaranteed to find it there in some small way, every day of the year.

Drumstick verbena (*Verbena bonariensis*) blooms in the garden of Jack Hyland and Larry Wente, Millerton, New York.

INTRODUCTION

Welcome to the Northeast! Whether you've lived here a few days, a few months, a few years, or your whole life, you're fortunate to be residing in one of the most exciting and dynamic regions of North America. Even better, if you've picked up this book, odds are you're planting a garden in the Northeast—and that is *truly* cause to celebrate. Yes, building a garden here (and anywhere) is a lot of work, but it's also one of the most rewarding endeavors you might undertake.

Small can be stunning, as in James Golden's garden in Brooklyn, New York.

More importantly, a little knowledge is key to building a garden, and this book seeks to arm you with that. First, we'll set the stage, with a little bit about the conditions we find ourselves gardening in here in the Northeast. From there, we'll survey a body of garden-worthy plants with which you can populate your northeastern landscape. (Hint: the possibilities are endless.) After that, the book will guide you through garden design, examining a group of gorgeous gardens in the Northeast through the scope of design elements and principles. Finally, we'll cover some of the hands-on aspects of growing things here, and what to expect when you're ready to get out there and get your hands dirty.

But wait—there's one more thing, and it may be more important than all the others. More than anything, these humble pages will seek to *inspire* you, not just in one chapter or section, but throughout the entire book. Why? Well, because gardening itself should be an inspiration. If your landscape is uninspired, it's time to change that. Let's get started.

The soothing sound of water is an ephemeral quality that helps create a strong sense of place in any garden.

ELEMENTS

Natural Forces That Shape Your Landscape

Spin your globe around to the part of North America where we live, and consider for a moment the parts that make the Northeast what it is. Yes, it can be plotted out in maps and legends, but these are man-made constructs. What about nor'easters and grains of sand, tidal pools and craggy peaks? The elements that make the Northeast distinct at the most basic level—our climate, our natural landscape—are especially important for us to understand as gardeners. We're all at the mercy of Mother Nature, but those of us who work with her to grow things tend to be more attuned to the change of the seasons, and the rhythms of our landscape's setting.

A shady vignette in the garden of Bob Scherer and Jeni Nunnally, York, Maine.

SEASONS

Four Faces of Our Region's Year

YOU'LL OFTEN HEAR that the Northeast "has" seasons. Most every place does, but given our place on the map, this speaks to how the differences between ours are more pronounced. Each season promises joys and headaches of its very own, but one thing's for sure: there's never a dull moment. Let's consider the Northeast's seasons in the garden.

SPRING

Most people think winter is the season that makes us come undone here in the Northeast, but my money's on spring. An average spring brings gradually warming temps and rain, the better to break bud. However, spring in the Northeast is also the most unpredictable of seasons, so a seasoned gardener knows to be ready for anything. Whereas the Northeast's other seasons tend to be relatively stable ("relatively," because our home is notorious for wild swings in weather), spring is the mood ring of seasons. Rather than a gradual warm-up, some springs jump ahead to 80 degrees and sunny, then plummet back to 40-degree gloom just in time for the weekend. Some springs see flooding from an overabundance of rain and snowmelt, while the occasional spring sees little rain at all. Hot or cold, wet or dry, spring isn't just a wakeup call to your garden from Mother Nature—it's a rallying cry to you, fellow gardener, to hop to it after a long, restless winter.

In places where the ground freezes tight, an integral part of spring is referred to as "mud season," because of the soil's sponginess after it thaws and then swells with spring rain.

Some of the best plants of spring are equally capricious. Bulbs are best known, and some of the first to bring bright color to the garden. They go hand in hand with plants we call spring ephemerals, a cast of characters that does all its blooming and growing before summer begins. Spring also sees most flowering trees do their thing for the year, as well as some popular seasonal shrubs.

Since it's the starting pistol for most plants to get growing, spring in the Northeast is a great season to plant new plants. Newcomers stimulated by rain and warming air and soil will be more likely to set down good roots.

EARLY TO MIDSUMMER

Summer in the Northeast is our personal horticultural reward for the hard work of making it through frigid winter and fickle spring. Thanks to our place

Tulips and hyacinths bloom in Central Park, New York.

on the map, we're fortunate enough to escape the more extreme heat much of the rest of North America sees—the stickiest humidity of summer in the South; the searing, drought- and fire-prone heat of the West. Summer in the Northeast usually means stretches of long, warm, sunny days, punctuated by periodic rainfall as humidity builds thunderstorms.

If spring is what kicks growing plants into gear, summer is when they hit their stride, and it's the time many an ornamental garden comes into its own. A menagerie of flowering shrubs and perennials blooms in the first half of summer, and warm-season annuals and tropicals can be added to instantly brighten gardens after frost dates have passed. Houseplants in containers head outside for a much needed "vacation."

Many blooming plants peak in the first half of summer, so a flower-focused ornamental garden can be a dog when the dog days hit. That's one reason you'll see many plants in this book recognized for their long season of interest, and why gardens that emphasize great foliage have gained in popularity.

Changing foliage of Japanese maple in the garden of Penny O'Sullivan, New Hampshire.

LATE SUMMER TO FALL

A Northeast summer reaches its zenith near July's end. The solstice has passed, and come August, those long days, though still hot, become noticeably shorter. Many ornamental gardens quiet down during this period, as if resting up for the beauty bonanza of fall. As the mercury peaks, the floral parade gives way to a simpler but more robust palette. Smoldering shades that foreshadow fall are the order of the day for late summer flowers (that's why I've grouped them with plants from that season), and late summer to autumn in these parts is the last hurrah for most flowering perennials. Rain and cooler temps prompt a new flush for some, while a small but forceful group waits to bloom, improbably, at the onset of fall. If conditions are just right, the first autumn foliage aligns with the last flowers in a magic hour that's almost unrivaled.

When fall does arrive, foliage is the order of the day, and deciduous woody plants are the true stars of that season. The Northeast is legendary for the fall color of its trees, and autumnal sweeps of red and yellow, gold and orange are synonymous with

Lilies in Chanticleer Garden, Wayne, Pennsylvania.

Osier dogwoods brighten the winter landscape in Maine.

the idea of our scenery. While a maple forest in October *is* truly stunning, there's a fall foliage plant for any size of garden, and the wise northern gardener fully partakes of this seasonal feature. Early autumn is also an excellent time to plant, as temperatures have cooled, rain is more frequent, and the soil is still warm.

After the raucous fall flush comes the most subtly beautiful botanical moment: a brief period characterized by an unmistakable stillness, after the last leaf has fluttered away, but before the first snow. The garden's bones take the stage for winter, the season we need them most.

WINTER

Cold, unforgiving, even brutal—these are words humans use to describe winter in the Northeast. The same holds true for plants, and the plants that survive here are remarkable in their hardiness. Winter varies wildly across the region: inland and northerly areas may well see a thick, consistent blanket of snow; those closer to the coast get swings from deep snow to near nothing; snow melts most quickly in the "heat islands" of Northeast cities.

All see frigid temperatures and winds to match. Snow is forever advertised as an excellent insulator for plants, and this is true—when the bottom falls out of the thermometer, a layer of snow is far better than bare ground. Snow becomes problematic when a thick layer begins to melt, refreezes, and becomes icy. Beware this freeze/thaw cycle, as it can mean burn for more tender evergreens and rot for plants that require sharp drainage. Wind makes itself known in winter more than other seasons as well, especially at coastal and high altitude sites. While winter wet can melt plants, winter winds can dry them to a crisp. Combat winter weather foes by getting to know your microclimates and siting plants carefully within them.

Conifers and a sturdy group of broadleaf evergreens are the belles of the winter ball, followed by leafless trees and shrubs with brightly colored bark, pretty berries, and intriguing form. The northeastern gardener's plant palette just for winter may seem slim, but in fact many plants that tend to be interesting over multiple seasons (see the Framework chapter) count winter as a time to shine.

GEOGRAPHY

Your Own Corner of the Northeast

THE FRENCH HAVE a term, *terroir*, which roughly translates to "sense of place." It's easy to get caught up in a frenzy of plant shopping and design and sail past that most basic garden question: Where do you live? Where exactly? A house on a busy street in the Philadelphia suburbs? A Maine cottage in a wooded area, a stone's throw from the water? A Brooklyn brownstone, a New Hampshire peak, or a Massachusetts cranberry bog? Even if your garden's site isn't as distinct as these examples, odds are it's got a touch of a few of them. Your garden's setting innately affects every aspect of what you can grow there, how it grows, and how you experience it—in work, in play, and as you move through it in your everyday life. Geographically, the Northeast is built out of a gallery of garden settings, both native and man-made. Each comes with unique challenges and rewards, and the most satisfied gardeners are those who learn to love the place their garden lives, and "don't fight the site." Since your garden probably has a dash of each, let's get a little acquainted with all of them to get to the bottom of what makes your garden tick.

A perennial garden in Greenland, New Hampshire.

COASTAL

The Atlantic Ocean acts as the eastern border of our region. Don't have waterfront property? Don't be so sure you're not coastal. Coastal areas include shoreline and near-coastal sites affected by tides—close to the mouths of tidal rivers, for example. Odds are, your garden could be closer to coastal than you think.

If you've ever gardened near big water, you know you can count on wind, sand, and salt. If you've got any or all, fear not! A host of tough plants thrive in coastal areas, as you'll see later in the book.

As with all oceans, it takes the Atlantic's waters a long time to respond to changes in air temperatures above. For coastal gardens, that translates to temps that are marginally milder in winter than their inland counterparts, but also slower to warm up in spring. Drying winds rob plants of valuable moisture, and many a coastal plant has evolved to work around wind. Likewise, coastal soils tend to be more sandy, with less organic material and less potential to retain moisture. Salt, another coastal constant, can also make seaside soil more alkaline, contrary to the acidic soil that is the standard in the Northeast. If you live near the ocean or a tidal river and see flooding during storms, salty water (called brackish water) can leave salt in your soil even after it drains away. Salt also comes in the more obvious

A meadow at Chanticleer Garden, Wayne, Pennsylvania.

form of salt spray, when the wind actually mists your garden from the Atlantic. Even if you live nowhere near the coast, it's good to know salt-tolerant plants because winter roads across our region are salted for safer driving, and the results can be the same. Fortunately, the same plants thrive in the shadow of a shoreline or salt truck.

Terrain often flattens out as you make the descent to sea level, and coastal areas are often more linear than other settings—a tantalizing hint to your inner compass that the Atlantic is just through the trees. Trees will typically be shorter where coastal winds blow with regularity, too. Everyone knows the coastal soundscape. Those waves may mean special challenges for you as a gardener, but the sound of them means your garden is automatically more relaxing than most.

MEADOW

In the hierarchy of wild places, some might argue meadows are the most untamed of all. Grasses make up the major botanical component of meadows, followed by wildflowers. Thanks to a few innovative landscape designers, the meadow garden is enjoying a resurgence in popularity, and rightfully so, as the meadow plant palette is one of the most exciting and ever changing over the course of the seasons.

Don't be fooled by meadows' carefree style: until

A collection of containers in New York City.

it's established, a meadow requires as much maintenance as many formal gardens (or more), because it's very easy for weeds to infiltrate that carefree planting plan. The elegantly unkempt meadow look can be a lot more work than most gardeners are cut out for.

Meadows may be wet or dry, and there are plants that work well in each, but one constant you'll usually find in a meadow environment is full sun—so much so that many meadow plants will bend toward the light in half-sun sites, and flop to the ground in shade. Because of the Northeast's history of farming, many a meadow today is yesterday's pasture, its soil rich from decades of amendment. By the same token, if your site was farmland recently, you may find yourself gardening in more depleted soil, with invasive species moving in to colonize.

Since terrain in the Northeast is naturally rolling, a meadow will often unfurl toward something in the distance—a woodland, a road, a distant neighbor. In context, meadows offer some of the best vistas around, their seasonal progression of plants a visual delight as they grow and change from week to week.

METROPOLITAN

You're probably familiar with the term "urban," but I think "metropolitan" is a better word to characterize a common set of conditions for gardeners in urban and suburban settings. The line between "downtown" and "suburb" is much less distinct in the Northeast than in some parts of the country. Cities here have concrete inner cores, usually with precious little green space for residents. These cores are enveloped by layers of suburbs, and yards gradually increase in size as you move outward from the urban core.

Temperature-wise, cities are heat islands, their vast stretches of pavement trapping the sun's rays and warming the air and soil around them. The closer you are to the urban core of a city, the higher the temperature will typically be.

Metropolitan soil is a smorgasbord in every way, but generally tends to be more disturbed than others. Building materials and road salt affect soil's chemical makeup, and it can often become lean and compacted. In disused sites, soil can contain all kinds of foreign objects. (Be sure to garden with gloves.) But even in suburbia, soil can be a surprise—often, when new homes are developed, topsoil is sold and carted away, so homeowners have to start fresh. Some builders put down loam, but unless it's supplemented with organic material like compost on a regular basis for several years afterward, the microscopic living things in soil that help plants thrive may not return naturally for a very long time. And speaking of that, since topsoil may have been taken away and added back to your metropolitan site, it could be wildly unlike your neighbor's. Soil testing is key.

Metro gardeners face some of the most interesting and varied cultural and design challenges. How to respond to the presence of thick black power lines in the view from your picture window? (Design your view to block, distract from, or accommodate them.) What to plant when your narrow plot gets shade through the a.m., but blasted by afternoon sun? (Tough plants that can take the twilight zone.) Intrusive sound can be especially challenging in metropolitan sites, traffic being the main offender. If you're bothered by traffic noise, consider adding a water feature—running water masks and distracts from many a racket. Likewise, the challenge of gardening between buildings can be much like gardening in a dry wooded site: full shade and low soil moisture. Dry shade plants are the answer. The payoff for metro gardens is that when thoughtfully planned and fearlessly planted they're an astounding surprise, not in spite of their setting, but because of it.

MOUNTAIN

Mountain sites are hard to pin down, but the one thing they have in common is shallow, sandy, rocky soil, low in organic material, and often on a slope where water doesn't stick around. "Rock garden" and "scree" are terms you may hear used for this kind of site, where topsoil can be thin and bedrock sits very close to the surface. New Hampshire, the Granite State, is especially known for this. Even so, an array of hardy herbaceous plants, shrubs, and even some trees are perfectly content to grow in rocky places, sinking their roots into crevices where others fear to tread. Many a mountain site also suffers harsh exposure to sun and wind, so the plants that thrive here grow just as well in tough man-made sites, too—in the cracks of a rock wall, for example, or sloping roadside sites. Soil along roadsides, in parking strips or "hellstrips," can become lean and compacted. While most gardeners' inclination is to overhaul the soil completely, there's a wealth of dryland plants that will grow in these most inhospitable of sites.

Succulents growing on a rocky site, Halls Pond Garden, Maine.

While mountain soil isn't always lean, the sites themselves tend to be more sloped, and for these gardens, guarding against erosion is the name of the game. Mountain gardeners will tell you stories of mulch and topsoil that wash downhill.

Mountain sites offer some of the most interesting topographical context for gardeners, and folks who truly garden in the mountains usually have the views we all envy most. Sure, you can plant whatever you want backing up to your view of the Presidential Range, where your soil allows, but wouldn't it be more interesting if your garden responded to that view?

WETLAND

Though water is the one thing all wetlands have in common, wet sites come in many forms: ponds, bogs, marshes, ditches, and the banks of streams and rivers. Some gardeners have the opportunity to design a garden around a pond or stream, but many, many more simply garden on sites in the neighborhood of a river, where the water table is high, and the rules are the same.

While every ecosystem has a cast of characters all its own, wetlands teem with life in a way few others can. All manner of mammal, bird, and insect are drawn to water. If you're a wildlife gardener in the market for a new home, look for the one with the pond out back—but look into your town's rules about wetlands before you appropriate one for your garden. Because native wetlands are so ecologically valuable, many cities and towns have rules as to how we can work around them, and it's no wonder. Weeding the average garden is challenge enough, but turn an invasive plant loose on the edge of a wetland, and you'll find yourself attempting to weed in waders. (It's a losing battle.) Of course, you can create a man-made water garden in a weekend with a pond kit, and you'll find it attracts wildlife in much the same way, especially if water resources are scarce in your area.

Pondside at Coastal Maine Botanic Gardens, Boothbay, Maine.

In soil, the wetland gardener's lot is obvious: plants should enjoy wet feet, or at least tolerate periodic inundation when rain is plentiful. Drainage is the watchword for wetland planting. Many plants prefer well-drained soil, meaning their roots may rot in soggy sites, and good drainage is hard to come by in true wetlands. Luckily, there's no shortage of gorgeous wetland plants that thrive in the Northeast.

Naturally occurring wetlands also tend to form in lowlands. In winter, cool air sinks and pools in these areas, so wetland temperatures tend to be on the lower side of their corresponding hardiness zone.

Wetlands can be tranquil and still—a large pond or marsh, for example—or, in the case of rivers and streams, a constant and soothing source of movement and sound. Wetland light and topography varies as much as wetlands themselves, but of the particular wildlife wetlands attract, frogs and insects tend to give wetlands a special evening soundtrack all their own.

WOODLAND

If you know trees, you know the Northeast boasts some of the most impressive native woodlands in the world. You may find yourself an inhabitant of a patch of woodland, or you may find your garden mimics woodland, if it's swathed in mature trees.

If there's one thing woodland gardeners hold most dear, it's light—shade gardening and woodland gardening are almost synonymous. If you're growing things that depend on light, be sure to monitor how the sun's rays move through your site as the day progresses, both during the growing season (when many plants will need it most) and in winter. For evergreens growing in the shade of deciduous trees, too much winter sun can be damaging.

Many years ago, the entire Northeast was blanketed by virgin woodland. The breakdown of leaves from those ancient trees—as well as trees today—is what gives us our typically acidic soil, high in organic matter. Soil on sites with mature trees will naturally be even more blessed with the decaying organic matter many plants love. Beyond the soil's makeup, soil moisture divides woodland gardens into two subsets: dry shade and damp. Many a woodland is prone to damp ground—organic matter in soil naturally absorbs and retains more water—and indeed, our mental picture of woodlands is often tranquil, still, and humid. Gardeners with damp shade, rejoice! Most "shade plants" will thrive for you. Those with dry shade know it's a much more challenging row to hoe in plant selection, but don't distress. Beautiful gardens grow in dry shade too, and I make mention in Part 2 of plants that do well on such sites.

Interestingly, woodland terrain and context vary in similar ways to metropolitan garden sites. Much the same as with buildings, light may not reach through the trees of your woodland site until, say, midday—then your plants get an extra-strength dose of sun. Maybe your woodland is primarily conifers, and shady year-round, or perhaps it's deciduous. It could be a mix of tall, mature trees and shorter understory trees and shrubs. One big plus for woodlands is sound. If it's serenity you're looking for in a garden, trees make for excellent natural acoustics. Woodlands are often serenely quiet in the daytime, and like wetlands, come alive at night with the sound of crickets and tree frogs.

A woodland area in the Brine Garden, New York.

PALETTE

Outstanding Plants for Northeast Gardens

Every landscape is a puzzle with many complex pieces, and plants, of course, are chief among them. In choosing plants, perhaps a better metaphor for landscape is that of a painting. If your yard is a canvas, and each new planting a brush stroke, it stands to reason that each plant is part of a palette.

A diversity of plant size, shape, texture, and color is on display in Maria Nation's garden in Sheffield, Massachusetts.

This section outlines that palette, and it's broken down into five chapters. First, we'll look in-depth at plants that put on some sort of show over the course of multiple seasons—even year-round. These plants make up the backbone of the garden, or framework. Then we'll move on to plants that take center stage in the parts of the year that correspond to those in the Seasons chapter: spring, early to midsummer, late summer to fall, and winter. For each plant (or group of plants), I'll touch on hardiness, size, and bloom period if it's a blooming plant. I'll also describe a number of other factors through these symbols:

FOLIAGE IS:	GROWS WELL IN:	SPECIAL CHARACTERISTICS:
EVERGREEN	SUN	SUPER HARDY (TO ZONE 4 OR LOWER)
SEMI-EVERGREEN	PART SUN	DEER-RESISTANT
DECIDUOUS D	PART SHADE	SALT-TOLERANT S
HERBACEOUS H	FULL SHADE	
NORTHEAST NATIVE SPECIES IN THE GENUS	WET SOIL	
	DRY SOIL	

Follow along for a survey of garden-worthy plants for the Northeast. Some may be familiar, and some may be old favorites, but you're guaranteed to find a few new hues to brighten up your landscape palette.

FRAMEWORK

Year-Round Landscape Backbone

While we often tend to think of garden plants through the scope of the four seasons, the wise gardener has in their horticultural palette a cadre of plants that do their thing over multiple seasons, or year-round. These workhorse plants make up the framework of the landscape, the basic skeleton of gardens. Incorporate them liberally into your plans, and you'll always be assured of something exciting just outside your door.

'Tricolor' beech (*Fagus* 'Tricolor') is colorful all through the growing season.

TREES, SHRUBS, AND VINES

Abies species and cultivars

Fir

HARDINESS: Zones 3/5–7

SIZE: 15–70 ft. high, 6–20 ft. wide

When it comes to evergreens, everybody's always talking about spruce and arborvitae. What about fir? Two specific types are just as sexy with more flexibility, and thrive in our humid summers and with a bit less sun.

'Silberlocke' Korean fir (*Abies koreana* 'Silberlocke').

Don't let white fir's name fool you: it's blue as they come, and easily passes for more popular Colorado blue spruce (*Picea pungens*), but white fir (*Abies concolor*, Zone 3) does that tree better, with more complex gradations of cyan to indigo. Established white fir grows 40-70 ft. high, and while it thrives with consistent moisture, this tree also makes a better candidate for dry sites in the Northeast than spruce. Want bluer still? Try cultivar 'Candicans'.

If you've got a thing for tinsel Christmas trees, 'Silberlocke' Korean fir (*Abies koreana* 'Silberlocke', Zone 5) could be the tree for you. This small fir dazzles with silver-bottomed needles that naturally curl upward like batting eyelashes, and grows 6-12 ft. high. Bonus: 'Silberlocke' decorates itself, albeit in spring, in cones that point straight up like toy soldiers, starting out chartreuse and aging to aubergine as the growing season progresses. Give firs well-drained soil and at least some sun, and they'll give back with a lifetime of evergreen goodness.

Acer species and cultivars

Japanese maple, moosewood, and paper bark maple

HARDINESS: Zones 3/4/5–9

SIZE: 10–30 ft. high and wide

D

Much like T-shirts, maples come in S, M, L, and XL. The big trees make for substantial presence year-round, but are truly awe-inspiring in fall, and I've included them in that section. Small to medium maples, however, play well in gardens of all types and sizes, and many are legendary for their colorfully filigreed multiseason foliage. All are as tough

TOP Moosewood (*Acer pensylvanicum*). ABOVE Japanese maple (*Acer japonicum* cultivar).

Paperbark maple (*Acer griseum*).

as they are beautiful, and as understory trees, thrive even in dry shade.

Paper bark maple (*Acer griseum*, Zone 4) must be the most unsung maple of all. This gracious tree sports distinctively feathery foliage, and its trunk and branches are coated in a glossy, exfoliating, russet-colored bark. It prefers a bit more sun than its cousins.

Better-known Japanese maple comes in a cornucopia of colors and leaf shapes. Most are cultivars of the species *Acer palmatum* (Zone 5), like familiar red-purple 'Bloodgood', and 'Sango-kaku', known as coral bark maple, which boasts bright red bark—a year-round treat, particularly in winter. The similar full moon maple (*A. shirasawanum*, Zone 5) has wide leaves that manage to be bold and finely textured all at once. 'Aureum' glows in the landscape.

These maples hail from other parts of the world. For a maple that's native and completely different, moosewood (*Acer pensylvanicum*, Zone 3) isn't just fun to say—it adores the cold and damp, but its bold foliage could pass for tropical. Grow it for that fab fall gold, and its reptilian bark, source of its other alias, snakebark maple. It prefers shade.

Actinidia kolomikta and cultivars

Hardy kiwi

HARDINESS: Zones 3/4–8

SIZE: 15–20 ft. high, 6–10 ft. wide

A vivacious climber, hardy kiwi struts its stuff with variegated leaves tipped in pink to white, an exotic treat as far north as Zone 4—Zone 3 in cultivar 'Arctic Beauty'. Male plants are the flashier gender when it comes to hardy kiwi, but it's the females that produce edible, grape-sized fruit if they're planted in pairs.

Hardy kiwi (*Actinidia kolomikta*).

Aristolochia macrophylla

Dutchman's pipe

HARDINESS: Zones 4–8

SIZE: 15–30 ft. high and wide

D

Want an easy swath of jungle in your damp Schenectady backyard? Dutchman's pipe is absolutely the vine for you. This wry climber wows with foot-long leaves, and makes itself at home on whatever structure it needs to reach for the sun. Give it medium to damp soil, and it's a cinch for fascinating foliage from spring to fall.

Dutchman's pipe (*Aristolochia macrophylla*).

Betula species and cultivars

Birch

HARDINESS: Zones 2/4–9

SIZE: 40–70 ft. high, 25–60 ft. wide

D

Here's the thing about birch: you may see it growing wild on dry, rocky outcrops alongside highways, but getting it to grow in your own dry yard will be more trouble than it's worth. Birch may grow in dry places if it decides to, but in general, and in cultivation, this picturesque tree much prefers damp. (Keep it clear of plumbing.) Birch revels in cold too, especially paper birch, which is too often planted in spots it despises. Unhappy trees planted on hot, dry sites contribute to the spread of a pest called bronze birch borer.

That said, few trees pack more visual punch year-round than paper birch (*Betula papyrifera*, Zone 2). This native tree's peely, papery bark has to be one of the purest non-floral whites in the plant kingdom. Resilient river birch (*B. nigra*, Zone 4) tolerates heat and humidity better than its cousin, and while it would rather grow in damp soil, it works in medium moisture conditions, too. River birch's cappuccino-colored trunks are coated in a chocolate crinoline of peeling outer bark. Another native, it's more prevalent in the Southeast, but its range extends to New England. Both birches do well with shade in the hottest part of the day, and paper birch thrives in the bitterest cold climates, where snow blankets the ground and keeps its roots clammy all winter. River birch often comes in a multi-trunked clump, and those with small gardens should look into cute cultivar 'Fox Valley', at 12 ft. high.

River birch (*Betula nigra*).

Buxus species and cultivars

Boxwood

HARDINESS: Zones 4–9

SIZE: 5–8 ft. high, 10–15 ft. wide; typically pruned smaller

Boxwood is a fixture in many landscapes, and indeed, this tiny-leaved shrub makes some of the best hedging around. It grows best in average, well-drained soil, and will take a bit of drought once established. Various cultivars of *Buxus sempervirens* and *B. microphylla* have been developed for greener foliage through winter, but it's best to expect a margin of bronzing. (Conifers may be a better choice for winter green.)

Boxwood (*Buxus* cultivar). RIGHT Heather (*Calluna* cultivar).

Calluna vulgaris cultivars, *Erica* species and cultivars

Heathers and heaths

HARDINESS: Zones 4–7

BLOOM PERIOD: Late winter, early spring, midsummer, late summer

SIZE: 1–2 ft. high and wide

S

A spate of pink heathers hit the market when these plants are in bloom, but otherwise, heathers are too often ignored by consumers. This is unfortunate, because these tiny, needle-leaved rhododendron relatives are fabulously tough and cold-hardy, thrive in the acidic soil of the Northeast, and make more interesting foliage evergreens than many a juniper. Of course, they bloom, too—heaths (*Erica*) late winter to spring, and heathers (*Calluna*) summer to fall. *C.* 'Orange Queen' is a favorite, with chartreuse foliage turning burnt orange in winter, while *E.* 'Winter Beauty' sports purple winter leaves with pink flowers. Heaths and heathers excel in seaside conditions.

Calycanthus floridus

Carolina allspice

HARDINESS: Zones 4–9

BLOOM PERIOD: Early summer, midsummer

SIZE: 6–10 ft. high, 6–12 ft. wide

Carolina allspice is best known for its best attribute: otherworldly burgundy flowers early to midsummer with the heady aroma of tropical fruit. What you may not have realized (and the reason it deserves a place in this chapter) is that this shrub has other charms, too. If you're a fan of tropical foliage, its big, glossy leaves won't disappoint—and even better, these turn a pretty yellow in fall. If it's fragrance you're after, shop for a plant in bloom, as it varies in intensity from shrub to shrub.

Carolina allspice (*Calycanthus floridus*).

Carpinus betulus and cultivars

European hornbeam

HARDINESS: Zones 4–8

SIZE: 40–60 ft. high, 30–40 ft. wide

D

The first name in garden framework is hornbeam, the silly putty of trees, more dynamic than most any other. This gem promises good green foliage and even better gray bark—a fine feature when winter rolls around. It grows in sun or shade, damp soil or dry. Left alone, it'll be a big, beautiful tree, but if you like, it shears superbly into a hedge. Tall, skinny cultivar 'Fastigiata' works even better for that purpose.

Fastigiate European hornbeam (*Carpinus betulus* 'Fastigiata').

Catalpa bignonioides, *C. speciosa*, and cultivars

Catalpa

HARDINESS: Zones 4–9

SIZE: 6–8 ft. high, 6 ft. wide, if pruned to the ground; 40–60 ft. high, 20–40 ft. wide, if left unpruned

Want to channel your inner punk into a plant? Catalpa is for you. A tree grown as a large shrub, it works best if chopped to the ground in late winter. When spring arrives, catalpa snaps back with new 6–8 ft. shoots lined with big, bawdy leaves. Southern catalpa (*Catalpa bignonioides*) is less hardy, to Zone 5, but gave birth to a bodacious bright-gold cultivar, 'Aurea'. Consider hardier northern catalpa (*C. speciosa*) for tropical flare in Zone 4. Catalpa makes a grand statement in small spaces.

'Aurea' catalpa (*Catalpa bignonioides* 'Aurea').

Cephalotaxus harringtonia cultivars

Plum yew

HARDINESS: Zones 6–10

SIZE: 5–10 ft. high and wide

Often overshadowed by its *Taxus* cousins, plum yew comes in two graceful types you should know: 'Fastigiata', a vertical, skinny, intricately layered shrub, perfect as an evergreen exclamation point in the garden; and its opposite, 'Prostrata', a yew that rolls and curtsies in needled waves along the ground. Both make stupendous evergreens in shade, where evergreenery can be a tall order. Plum yew is typically hardy in protected sites of Zone 5.

Prostrate plum yew (*Cephalotaxus harringtonia* cultivar).

Cercidiphyllum japonicum and cultivars

Katsura

HARDINESS: Zones 4–8

SIZE: 40–60 ft. high, 25–60 ft. wide

D ☀ ◐ 🌡

Katsura is such an overachiever you'll be hard pressed to pick a favorite trait. The loosely linear arrangement of its branches and heart-shaped leaves is a geometric delight. Its trunk and surface roots become ornately furrowed with age. Its red-gold fall foliage may be most tantalizing of all, but not for color—when they turn and fall to the ground, those autumn leaves carry with them the scent of cinnamon.

Katsura (*Cercidiphyllum japonicum*).

Chamaecyparis species and cultivars

False cypress

HARDINESS: Zones 4/5–8

SIZE: 3–25 ft. high, 4–12 ft. wide

Another group of indispensible conifers for the garden framework, cultivars of false cypress (also called hinoki cypress) come in more different shapes, sizes, and colors than any other. All would opt for more sun than arborvitae, but take more shade than juniper. All prefer soil of medium moisture, but established plants weather periods of drought with no problem.

In shrubs, it's tough to beat dwarf hinoki cypress (*Chamaecyparis obtusa* 'Nana Gracilis', Zone 4), with its oddly geometric, whorled foliage. For brighter color and finer texture try a variety of gold threadleaf false cypress, like *C. pisifera* 'Golden Mop' (Zone 5). In time, both of these grow to 3–6 ft. in height, and 4–5 ft. wide.

For a tree-sized false cypress, look no further than hinoki cultivar 'Crippsii' (Zone 4), a shimmering coniferous vision year-round, but especially during the dark, chilly days of winter. It grows into a small tree, 12–25 ft. tall, and prefers sun. If gold is too bold, try weeping Alaskan cedar (*Chamaecyparis nootkatensis* 'Pendula', Zone 4), the classic cone-shaped conifer enhanced, its pendulous arms conjuring images of fairytale forests year-round. It's a bit larger, growing 20–35 ft., prefers shade in the heat of the day, and its species is sometimes called *Xanthocyparis*.

Gold threadleaf false cypress (*Chamaecyparis pisifera* 'Golden Mop').

'Crippsii' hinoki cypress (*Chamaecyparis obtusa* 'Crippsii').

Cotinus coggygria cultivars

Smoke tree

HARDINESS: Zones 4–8

BLOOM PERIOD: Early summer, midsummer

SIZE: 10–15 ft. high and wide

D

Fans of purple will want to be sure to plant smoke tree, a plant so purple it verges on black. Smoke tree gets its name from its flowers, which also produce billowy pink tufts of hair after they've faded, like cotton candy. If you're looking for this "smoke," keep pruning to a minimum, but for more foliage, this shrub can be cut back dramatically in late winter, prompting giant new shoots with bigger leaves. 'Royal Purple' is a classic cultivar, but fans of gold leaves should check out 'Golden Spirit'. Smoke tree is drought-resistant, and thrives even in lean soils.

Purple smoke tree (*Cotinus coggygria* cultivar).

RIGHT Variegated wintercreeper (*Euonymus fortunei* 'Coloratus').

Euonymus fortunei and cultivars

Wintercreeper

HARDINESS: Zones 4–9

SIZE: 1–3 in. high, indefinite spread

Wintercreeper is like wall-to-wall garden carpet: you may hate it until you see the need for it. This viney evergreen grows most anywhere, and makes a great problem-solver for uniform groundcover in dense, dry shade. Its super-creepy habit of blanketing all the ground it's allowed means it works best with big trees and shrubs, and only the most robust of perennials. Keep an eye out in case it decides to climb—it will scale trees or structures if you let it. Popular cultivars include winter-bronze 'Coloratus', white-edged 'Variegatus', and gilt 'Emerald 'n' Gold'.

Fagus sylvatica and cultivars

European beech

HARDINESS: Zones 4–7

SIZE: 20–60 ft. high, 20–50 ft. wide

D

So you're gardening someplace with room to grow, and you've decided to give a mammoth tree a home. Congratulations! No giant tree is more genteel than European beech, and none more colorful than copper beech, cultivar 'Purpurea'. If giant purple trees just aren't dazzling enough, 'Tricolor' beech is for you. This cultivar's leaves aren't just purple, they're edged in a wild pink-to-white gradient. At a more polite 25–30 ft. tall and wide, 'Tricolor' also fits well into gardens that aren't the size of golf courses. Beeches may grow into behemoths, but they do best with a bit of shade in their formative years, as well as soil that's not overly wet or dry.

Fargesia species and cultivars

Clumping bamboo

HARDINESS: Zones 5–9

SIZE: 6–15 ft. high, 8–12 ft. wide

Bamboos are huge grasses, but they're woody like shrubs, and their size means you can treat them as such in the garden framework. While running bamboos spread famously to form groves, clumpers like hardy *Fargesia* offer the same bamboo ambience and stick where you plant them. All prefer medium to moist soil but tolerate dry, and all do best with shade in the heat of the day. For tight spaces, try red-stemmed *F.* 'Jiuzhiagou', which grows to 15 ft. with a width less than half that. Shorter *F. rufa* tops out at 8 ft., but stretches its wings to the same width. *F. murielae* is similar but bigger, at 12 ft. tall and wide. Clumping bamboos grow slowly, so invest in a big plant or give it some time to fill out.

Clumping bamboo (*Fargesia rufa*). LEFT 'Tricolor' beech (*Fagus sylvatica* 'Tricolor').

Fothergilla species and cultivars

Fothergilla

HARDINESS: Zones 4–8

BLOOM PERIOD: Midspring, late spring

SIZE: 3–10 ft. high and wide

D

Its name may be a tongue twister, but folks in the know see fothergilla as a multifaceted, multiseason star for shade. This plant blooms with honey-scented white cylinders in spring, ends the season with flaming red-orange fall color, and various cultivars promise interesting foliage in between. Large fothergilla (*Fothergilla major*) grows to 10 ft., while a dwarf species (*F. gardenii*) tops out at 4. For the most vavoom between spring and fall, *F. gardenii* 'Blue Mist' and hybrid *F.* ×*intermedia* 'Blue Shadow' both sport a leafy patchwork in hues from silver to powder blue.

Fothergilla (*Fothergilla* cultivar).

Gaultheria procumbens

Wintergreen

HARDINESS: Zones 3–8

SIZE: 4–6 in. high, 6–12 in. wide

Looking for an easy groundcover, an edible, an evergreen, or a native plant? How about all four? Wintergreen grows naturally in woodlands of eastern North America, and this woody groundcover's leaves can be used to make a tea. Its minty berries are forage for wildlife of all kinds—you can eat them, too—and it thrives in acidic soil in shade that's a bit damp or dry.

Wintergreen (*Gaultheria procumbens*).

Gleditsia triacanthos var. *inermis* cultivars

Honeylocust

HARDINESS: Zones 3–9

SIZE: 40–50 ft. high, 30–40 ft. wide

Thornless honeylocust is the tough-as-nails tree that brings elegance to even the most abused of hell-strips. It's also a chameleon—its branch structure and tiny, glossy leaves reminiscent of the acacias of the African savannah, its lineage purely of American forests. Honeylocust's trunk grows into a pillar of textured concrete with age, and its open canopy makes it an ideal tree for underplanting.

Honeylocust (*Gleditsia triacanthos* var. *inermis*).

Hedera helix and cultivars

English ivy

HARDINESS: Zones 4–9

SIZE: 20–80 ft. high, 10–50 ft. wide

Don't be afraid of English ivy—just be smart when it comes time to plant. An impenetrable groundcover or wallcover, evergreen ivy excels given license to do what we all know it does best: spread out. Plant ivy as a singular feature, or with shrubs that can compete. Beware its tendency to treat trees like a stairway to heaven, and especially to run amok in milder Zone 7.

English ivy (*Hedera helix*).

Hydrangea anomola subsp. *petiolaris*, *Schizophragma hydrangeoides* and cultivars

Climbing hydrangea

HARDINESS: Zones 4–9

BLOOM PERIOD: Midsummer, late summer

SIZE: 30–50 ft. high, 5–9 ft. wide

D ☀ ☼ ◐ ☁ ≡ 🌡 🦌 S

Don't let their botanical names fool you: two plants go by the common name "climbing hydrangea," and they both do great things in the framework of the dry shade garden. Not content to be ground dwellers, these hydrangeas take to the air. The white flowers of *Hydrangea anomola* subsp. *petiolaris* may be more blousy than those of *Schizophragma*, but two great varieties of the second plant up the ante: pink-flowered 'Roseum' and silvery blue-leaved 'Moonlight', a shimmering three-season gem in shade. These big woody vines get vertical via aerial rootlets, so site them on something permanent. A freestanding stone wall works well; mortared walls of homes that will need to be repointed may not be a good choice. Climbing hydrangea starts slow, then takes off, and blooms in masses of white clouds in summer. Glossy new leaves add foliar interest to the mix.

'Moonlight' climbing hydrangea (*Schizophragma hydrangeoides* 'Moonlight').

Ilex species and cultivars

Holly

HARDINESS: Zones 4–9

SIZE: 4–20 ft. high, 4–15 ft. wide

While there are conifers aplenty for Northeast gardens, five-star broadleaf evergreens for cold climates can be hard to come by. Hollies are the workhorses in that category where we live. (One notable holly, winterberry, loses its leaves, but excels in that season all the same.) All hollies are versatile plants, and tough enough to pay their way in the framework of any great northern garden.

If there's one holly that's overused in the Northeast landscape, it's Japanese holly (*Ilex crenata*, Zone 6/warmer parts of Zone 5). This tough plant's tidy nature means it's the fallback for many a formal planting in our part of the country—that said, if planted creatively and pruned correctly, it's as prim as any boxwood, and can be worth the hype. 'Sky Pencil' (or 'Sky Sentry') is a standout, growing arrow-straight as tall as 8 ft. Other common types include dwarves 'Helleri' and 'Soft Touch', both of which grow to 4 ft. For something similar in a native plant, try inkberry (*I. glabra*, Zone 4), a popular alternative with tiny black berries in fall, great for bird gardens. It's also hardier and more deer-resistant. Inkberry tends to get leggy if not pruned regularly—for denser plants, try cultivars 'Shamrock' or 'Compacta'.

For those in search of the "holliest" of hollies, blue holly (*Ilex* ×*meserveae*, Zone 4) cuts a figure most reminiscent of less-hardy English holly (*I. aquifolium*, Zone 6). Glinting leaves in forest green are less prickly than its UK cousin, and always impeccably neat. Be sure to plant male and female cultivars for those famed fall-to-winter red berries.

'Sky Pencil' Japanese holly (*Ilex crenata* 'Sky Pencil').
BELOW Inkberry (*Ilex glabra*).

They may be tough, but blue hollies are best sited away from drying winter winds, and grow to 10 ft. if unpruned.

Want to try a holly that's most underused? Longstalk holly (*Ilex pedunculosa*, Zone 5) makes an outstanding foundation plant, so named for galaxies of red berries suspended from its branches from fall into winter. A bonus is pretty leaves that'll have the neighbors wondering why you planted your houseplant weeping fig (*Ficus benjamina*) outdoors. As usual, you'll need male and female plants for fruit.

Blue holly (*Ilex* ×*meserveae*).

Juniperus species and cultivars

Juniper

HARDINESS: **Zones 2/3/4–9**

SIZE: **6 in.–20 ft. high, 5–15 ft. wide**

The lowly juniper—often maligned, unquestionably useful . . . but beautiful? That's right, juniper isn't just for median strips anymore. This tough genus doesn't just tolerate blazing sun and dry, rocky soil—it says bring it on. Some junipers creep, some spread, and some grow into trees.

'Gold Coast' juniper (*Juniperus* ×*pfitzeriana* 'Gold Coast').

Taller spreading junipers need space to stretch their wings in the landscape, but some are worth it for color, like sparkly *Juniperus* ×*pfitzeriana* 'Gold Coast' (Zone 4). Another star is a cultivar of native eastern red cedar, *J. virginiana* 'Grey Owl' (Zone 2), a glinting, glimmering evergreen that puts those parking lot plants to shame. These two typically top out around 4 ft., but if you're in the market for something taller, try red cedar cultivar 'Taylor' (Zone 3), a skinny, columnar tree that grows to 20 ft.

Of the creeping junipers, *Juniperus squamata* 'Blue Star' (Zone 4) steals the show. Its intricate needles catch light individually, like tiny cerulean prisms, and this easy groundcover goes well with just about everything. Give it sun and any old non-soggy soil and it's a happy camper. Those in need of a similarly coniferous groundcover that takes light shade should also consider a creeping juniper lookalike called Siberian cypress (*Microbiota decussata*, Zone 3). This tough green spreader turns a coppery bronze in winter.

'Blue Star' juniper (*Juniperus squamata* 'Blue Star').

Koelreuteria paniculata

Golden rain tree

HARDINESS: Zones 5–9

BLOOM PERIOD: Midsummer, late summer

SIZE: 30–40 ft. high and wide

D

Golden rain tree gets going in summer and scarcely skips a beat until frost. First up are frothy clouds of yellow flowers that later drop, hence its common name, a prelude to coral lanterns that hold the tree's seeds. Add finely cut foliage that turns orange-gold in fall, and there's got to be a reason for you to grow golden rain tree. This small tree thrives in sun and dry to average soil, a perfect fit curbside.

Golden rain tree (*Koelreuteria paniculata*).

Leucothoe fontanesiana cultivars

Leucothoe

HARDINESS: Zones 5–9

BLOOM PERIOD: Late spring

SIZE: 2–6 ft. high, 4–6 ft. wide

It's a little tough to say, and maybe that's why leucothoe (pron. "loo-co-tho-EE") gets short shrift in gardens, but this elegant evergreen dazzles in deer-prone dry shade. Planted with bold-leaved perennials, it looks downright exotic, and its spreading nature makes it an ideal groundcover to boot. Foliage of variegated 'Rainbow' is splattered in white to pink, while 'Scarletta' swoons in red.

Leucothoe (*Leucothoe fontanesiana* cultivar).

Magnolia species and cultivars

Magnolia

HARDINESS: Zones 5–10

BLOOM PERIOD: Late spring, early summer

SIZE: 10–40 ft. high and wide

In the Northeast, most magnolias bloom raucously in spring before fading into obscurity the rest of the year. Most magnolias, that is, except for a few notable groups that keep the party going late and loud: bigleaf magnolias (best as foliage plants) and sweet bay for both leaf and flower. Both grow perfectly in damp to medium and, in some cases, even moderately dry soil. In our climate, both will be better with protection from wind, especially in Zone 5.

Two easy-to-grow species of bigleaf magnolia grow in the Northeast, beloved by those in the know for rafts of leaves the likes of banana. Southern native *Magnolia macrophylla*'s leaves are bigger—up to 30 in.—and subject to shredding like banana. Plant it in the lee of a house or windbreak to be safe. Leaves of *M. tripetala* may be smaller, but at 24 in. still give tender tropicals a run for their money. A vigorous understory tree whose home range extends into the Northeast, it grows well, if more slowly, even in dry shade. You may miss its spring flowers, but rose-pink cones in fall stop traffic.

Sweet bay (*Magnolia virginiana*) makes a stellar small tree in flower and leaf. Like its namesake true bay (*Laurus nobilis*), its silver-bottomed foliage smells spicy when crushed—but unlike bay, it's just for scent, not for eating. Like its bigger cousins, it blooms, but in early summer, with dove-textured white flowers that send a lemon scent into the air. Unlike other hardy mags, many of its waxy mid-green leaves hold through winter. Varieties 'Moonglow' and *M. virginiana* var. *australis* up the ante on evergreenery.

Sweet bay magnolia (*Magnolia virginiana*).

Metasequoia glyptostroboides

Dawn redwood

HARDINESS: Zones 4–8

SIZE: 70–100 ft. high, 15–25 ft. wide

D

If there's one tree that's surprisingly underused, it's this tree. Reminiscent of baldcypress (*Taxodium distichum*), dawn redwood also grows into a pleasingly green, cone-shaped conifer, with soft, deciduous needles that turn a russet color in fall. The bonus with this tree is a trunk straight out of Middle Earth: a fluted pillar of intricately textured red buttresses with age. Like baldcypress, dawn redwood also works well in wet spots, but even excels as a street tree. Even more spectacular is cultivar 'Ogon', also called 'Gold Rush', which features sungold foliage.

Myrica species and cultivars

Bayberry

HARDINESS: Zones 3–7

SIZE: 5–10 ft. high and wide

D

A wilder alternative to ho-hum holly, bayberry is a steel-tough plant with steely blue fruit. Semi-evergreen in the warmer parts of its range, this fragrant-leaved native adapts to damp soils or dry, and adores salt spray, making it a must-have in the coastal garden framework. Male and female plants are a must-have as well, for BB-sized fruit that serves as food for birds.

Bayberry (*Myrica pensylvanica*). LEFT 'Ogon' dawn redwood (*Metasequoia glyptostroboides* 'Ogon').

Physocarpus opulifolius cultivars

Ninebark

HARDINESS: Zones 2–8

BLOOM PERIOD: Late spring, early summer

SIZE: 4–8 ft. high and wide

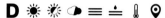

D

Native ninebark was a pretty obscure shrub until the arrival of a crayon box of colorfully leaved cultivars, in shades ranging from cheery gold to black-purple to smoldering red. Now is ninebark's time, and thank goodness, because this hearty shrub is just the ticket for multiseason color in just about any sunny spot (its foliage color will fade in shade). Reds include 'Center Glow' and dwarf, tiny-leaved 'Little Devil'. 'Diabolo' is deepest maroon, while 'Coppertina' grades from gold to orange to red-purple. 'Dart's Gold' is the granddaddy of them all.

'Diabolo' ninebark (*Physocarpus opulifolius* 'Diabolo').

Picea species and cultivars

Spruce

HARDINESS: Zones 2/3/4–7

SIZE: 3–60 ft. high, 2–20 ft. wide

S

Spruces sparkle in gardens of the Northeast, but not all spruces are created equal. Some grow into huge trees, but some delight as lively garden shrubs. Give them full sun and medium moisture in youth, and you'll be rewarded with a first-class conifer.

'Skylands' spruce (*Picea orientalis* 'Skylands').

A layered green meringue of a shrub, bird's nest spruce (*Picea abies* 'Nidiformis' and others, Zone 3) makes a fascinating accent, its stacked branches puddling out in a pool of evergreen. It only grows to 3 ft. high and 5 ft. wide. Tree-sized 'Skylands' spruce (*P. orientalis* 'Skylands', Zone 4), on the other hand, grows into a classically coniferous 35-ft. pyramid. Rather than plain green, its short needles are gold. Like the others, it's best in sun, but a smidge of shade in the heat of the day won't slow it down, and its gold will be less likely to bleach out. Shelter 'Skylands' from harsh winter winds in the northern reaches of its range.

Colorado blue spruce (*Picea pungens*, Zone 2) is the most popular member of the spruce clan, and given its fabulous ice-blue foliage, it's easy to see why. Make blue spruce happy, and it's a snap to grow. Too much shade or drought, as a young tree, and it's a spider mite metropolis. Blue spruce needs room, growing 30–60 ft. high and 10–20 ft. wide. Many homeowners plant it as a living Christmas tree, never considering its ultimate heft. For most, the "dwarf" cultivar 'Fat Albert' makes a great garden addition, topping out at a modest 10–15 ft. high and 7–10 ft. wide. Those in search of a truly dwarf Colorado blue should consider shrubby 'Glauca Globosa', a botanical star topping out around 5 ft. tall and wide.

Colorado blue spruce (*Picea pungens*).

Pinus species and cultivars

Pine

HARDINESS: Zones 2/3/4–8

SIZE: 5–80 ft. high, 5–40 ft. wide

A staple among evergreens, pines are perhaps the most well known of their needly clan. Giant native white pine (*Pinus strobus*, Zone 3) may be best known in the Northeast, and its soft, bluish foliage is a welcome sight year-round. Though it will grow 80 ft. tall in time, it can be sheared to shape—even trained as a hedge—and cultivars come in many shapes and sizes, from prostrate to fastigiate. It puts up with dry soil less well than its cohorts.

Other notable trees include lacebark pine (*Pinus bungeana*, Zone 4), a star with white-mottled bark that grows 30–50 ft. For smaller gardens, *P. flexilis* 'Vanderwolf's Pyramid' (Zone 4) makes a pyramidal statement with blue needles, or try the deep forest tones of narrow 'Oregon Green' Austrian pine (*P. nigra* 'Oregon Green', Zone 4). Both grow to around 25 ft.

All these trees are drought-resistant once well established, but for those with tougher soil and less space, mugo pine (*Pinus mugo*, Zone 2) is the evergreen answer. This little pine is a steam engine, usually no more than 6 ft., with cultivars like tiny 'Teeny' topping out around 1 ft. Each plant resembles a whole forest of conifers in miniature.

Mugo pine (*Pinus mugo*).

White pine (*Pinus strobus*).

Quercus species and cultivars

Oak

HARDINESS: Zones 3/4–9

SIZE: 50–75 ft. high, 40–75 ft. wide

D

If you've got a spot for a big tree and want to plant for wildlife, look no further than oak. Famous for many reasons, but especially for their acorns, oaks are said to provide more value to woodland creatures big and small than most any other tree—especially because animals love acorns. You, however, may not love acorns in spots where you walk barefoot or park your car, so keep this in mind when planting. Natives red oak (*Quercus rubra*) and scarlet oak (*Q. coccinea*) are go-tos for dry soil and fabulous fall crimson. Pin oak (*Q. palustris*) and swamp white oak (*Q. bicolor*, Zone 3) excel in wet soil.

Oak (*Quercus* species).

Rhus species and cultivars

Sumac

HARDINESS: Zones 3–9

BLOOM PERIOD: Midsummer

SIZE: 2–25 ft. high, 6–30 ft. wide

D

No, it's not poison, and yes, you're missing out if you're not growing it. Ornamental sumac isn't only a native plant—it's a must for fabulous foliage and form year-round, and thrives even in poor, sun-blasted sites. Staghorn sumac (*Rhus typhina*) grows tall, and features symmetrical, palm-like crowns.

'Gro-Low' sumac (*Rhus aromatica* 'Gro-Low').

'Tiger Eyes' staghorn sumac (*Rhus typhina* 'Tiger Eyes').

Fall color comes in fire engine red, and in late summer, female plants sport pointy, cone-like clusters of red fruit that last through winter. Cultivar 'Tiger Eyes' takes it a step further, with chartreuse leaves through the growing season. If you're more in the market for groundcover than tree, try 'Gro-Low' sumac, a spreading cultivar of *R. aromatica*, with buttercream spring flowers and small, shiny leaves that turn deep red in fall. Sumacs are colonizers, so it's best to give them space.

Salix species and cultivars

Willow

HARDINESS: Zones 2–9

SIZE: **4–80 ft. high, 5–70 ft. wide**

D ☀ ◐ ≐ 🌡 🦌 S

Willows exude an air of shabby chic and easy elegance we'd all love for our yards. Large willows, like weeping willow (*Salix alba* 'Tristis' or *S. babylonica*, Zone 2), are the grand dames of the willow clan, and great for wet sites—the movement of their small leaves gives the sense there's a pond in the garden even when there isn't. Big willows can be a challenge to site because they can grow up to 80 ft. tall, litter their nests with twigs and leaves, and their busy root systems sniff out water like bloodhounds. (Read: plant nowhere near plumbing.) Fear not, gardeners lacking in space! There's a willow for every size garden.

Colorful dappled willow (*Salix integra* 'Hakuro-nishiki', Zone 5) starts the growing season with white-speckled foliage, splashed liberally in pink. It will grow to 8 ft., but is easily trained, and established plants can be cut back hard in late winter to promote more colorful new growth. Smaller, 5-ft. arctic blue willow (*S. purpurea* 'Nana', Zone 4) has icy foliage and stays shrubby. It benefits

Weeping willow (*Salix* species). BELOW Dappled willow (*Salix integra* 'Hakuro-nishiki').

from regular hard pruning as well. Perhaps the most underused willow of all is rosemary willow (*S. elaeagnos*, Zone 4), a decadent color accent with shimmering silver foliage, and reminiscent of olive, for northern gardeners in search of Mediterranean chic. It can be grown as a tree, up to 12 ft., or easily kept to shrub size.

Arctic blue willow (*Salix purpurea* 'Nana').

Sambucus species and cultivars

Elderberry

HARDINESS: Zones 3/4–9

BLOOM PERIOD: Midsummer

SIZE: 15–25 ft. high, 10 ft. wide

D ☀ ◐ ≐ 🌡 S ⚲

With foliage cultivars in purple and gold that make colorful framework across the growing season, lacy elderberry answers the Japanese maple craving in zones too cold for that plant. *Sambucus nigra* 'Black Lace' and 'Black Beauty' (Zone 4) are two purples—they bloom pink, too—while *S. racemosa* 'Sutherland Gold' comes in sunny yellow. Hardy to Zone 3, the green native species *S. canadensis* is all about bubbling bouquets of summer white, and purple fruit fit for jams and pies. Elderberries adapt just fine to a range of soil types, but they'll love you best if your garden is damp.

'Black Lace' elderberry (*Sambucus nigra* 'Black Lace').

Spiraea species and cultivars

Spirea

HARDINESS: **Zones 4–8**

BLOOM PERIOD: **Midspring, early summer, midsummer**

SIZE: **2–5 ft. high, 3–5 ft. wide**

D

A workhorse among shrubs, vivacious spirea grows as well in parking lots as parterres. It blooms pink to white, with cultivars in a range of foliage choices, some sporting eye-popping pink flowers and citron leaves all at the same time. One standout beats the rest by a mile: 'Ogon' spirea (*Spiraea thunbergii* 'Ogon', Zone 4), also sold as 'Mellow Yellow'. This plant hits spring like the others, with billows of white bridal wreath bloom, but for 'Ogon', that's the party preview. It follows up with willowy, glittering gold-to-lime leaves, a sight throughout the growing season well into fall—then they turn tangerine. Among other types, *S. japonica* 'Goldflame' and 'Gold Mound' make neat, lemony globes all season. For a more understated look, go with 'Tor' birchleaf spirea (*S. betulifolia* 'Tor'), a confection with white snowball flowers, and tiers of circular leaves that turn a jaw-dropping fall red. Give spirea mostly sun and it adapts to most soils and situations. For the deer-prone garden, it medals in gold.

'Ogon' spirea (*Spiraea thunbergii* 'Ogon').

Stephanandra incisa 'Crispa'

Stephanandra

HARDINESS: Zones 3–8

SIZE: 1–3 ft. high, 1–4 ft. wide

D

A spreading solution for slopes and dry shade, stephanandra may be a mouthful, but it's a sure thing as a polite groundcover, especially if you're nervous about ivy or wintercreeper and don't need evergreen. This plant prefers average to moist soil, but swings mild drought just fine with shade in the heat of the day. Sited on slopes, it's a gurgling fountain of green, turning orange-yellow in fall. Pretty cutleaf cultivar 'Crispa' is likely what you'll find for sale.

Stephanandra (*Stephanandra incisa* 'Crispa').

Taxodium distichum and cultivars

Baldcypress

HARDINESS: Zones 4–9

SIZE: 50–70 ft. high, 25–40 ft. wide

D

You may know baldcypress as a tree of southern swamps, but this dynamic conifer happens to be completely cold-hardy and so drought-resistant they grow it in traffic islands in Texas—a far droughtier place than any in our climate. Besides that, this picturesque, pyramidal deciduous conifer is known for its beautiful bark and orange fall color. Straight and narrow 'Shawnee Brave' is one great cultivar.

Baldcypress (*Taxodium distichum*).

Taxus species, hybrids, and cultivars

Yew

HARDINESS: Zones 4–7

SIZE: 2–25 ft. high and wide; typically pruned smaller

Whether yours IDs as English (*Taxus baccata*), Japanese (*T. cuspidata*), or a cross of the two (*T.* ×*media*), workhorse yew makes evergreen elegance easy. Tolerant of conditions across the board, wet soil may be the only place yew won't do. Yews are champs in dry shade, and upright varieties make some of the best hedging around—be sure to prune before new growth shows up in spring. If yews have one downfall, it's that deer love them too.

Yew (*Taxus* species).

Thuja species and cultivars

Arborvitae

HARDINESS: Zones 2/3/5–8

SIZE: 4–60 ft. high, 5–18 ft. wide

Arborvitae is a venerable evergreen whose name means "tree of life," so it's ironic that it's abused nearly as often as it's used: badly sheared into unsightly hedges, left unpruned to gobble up whole homes, pretty until the deer get the munchies. Don't blame arborvitae—plant it smartly. Of its varied cultivars, a few standouts take to the role of hedge, screen, or even specimen plant with flying colors. All prove adaptable but prefer mostly sun and soil of medium moisture.

When it comes to beefy screen, *Thuja* 'Green Giant' is an A-1 evergreen. This arborvitae grows more quickly than most, and given the sun and space, forms an immense, inverted cone, perfect for a privacy hedge. Even better, 'Green Giant' gets two thumbs up in shade, and (unlike most) two thumbs

'Green Giant' arborvitae (*Thuja* 'Green Giant').

down for deer on the hunt for a meal. For small spaces or as a repeated motif in larger landscapes, skinny *T. occidentalis* 'Degroot's Spire' makes a striking, if soft, exclamation, at more than 20 ft. high and less than 6 ft. wide. Staggered along a fence line, this cultivar of native white cedar makes an excellent screen—tall but shallow.

Bored with these ho-hum evergreens? *Thuja plicata* 'Whipcord' (Zone 5) is an arborvitae with dreadlocks. 'Whipcord' starts life looking more grass-like than shrub-like, but in time grows into a mid-sized green mop of fine-textured foliage. If you'd rather a more colorful option, try fizzy needly *T. occidentalis* 'Golden Tuffet' (Zone 3), a bubbly mini-evergreen at 2 ft. tall.

Tilia cordata

Littleleaf linden

HARDINESS: **Zones 3–8**

SIZE: **50–70 ft. high, 35–50 ft. wide**

D ☀ ◐ ≡ 🌡

Some time after summer really sets in, a sweet, soapy perfume mysteriously fills the air, even along gritty city sidewalks: lindens, blooming with small yellow flowers, all the better for people and bees. This mid-sized tree isn't just great for fragrance—its leathery green leaves make a neat garden backdrop throughout the growing season, and turn bright gold in fall. Left alone, linden grows into a neat beehive shape, but it can even be trimmed into a hedge.

Littleleaf linden (*Tilia cordata*).

Tsuga canadensis

Canadian hemlock

HARDINESS: Zones 3–7

SIZE: 40–70 ft. high, 25–35 ft. wide

A cold, damp hemlock is a happy hemlock. This majestic tree can be among the most valuable evergreens for screening, and for the inhospitable north side of a house, where moisture and chill prevail. Give it room to spread and plan to underplant sparely in maturity, as hemlock shade is notoriously dry. Since the 1950s, hemlock has been plagued by woolly adelgid (*Adelges tsugae*), an exotic insect pest. Hemlocks planted on hot, droughty, windy sites are more likely to be infested, further endangering native populations.

Canadian hemlock (*Tsuga canadensis*).

Ulmus americana 'Valley Forge'

'Valley Forge' American elm

HARDINESS: Zones 5–9

SIZE: 60–70 ft. high, 50–60 ft. wide

D

Since the 1930s, Dutch elm disease, an exotic pest, has decimated native American elm populations. Once one of our most beloved national trees, elms all but disappeared. Undaunted horticulturists selected the most disease-resistant among the surviving population, and 'Valley Forge' is the best of the bunch. Graceful giants, elms are the tall, cool drink of water among trees, prized for their vase-like structure—an asset to any garden's bones. This tree is likely hardy to Zone 4, but tested to Zone 5.

'Valley Forge' American elm (*Ulmus americana* 'Valley Forge').

Vaccinium angustifolium and cultivars, *V. corymbosum* cultivars

Blueberry

HARDINESS: Zones 3–8

SIZE: 1–12 ft. high and wide

D ☀ ◐ 🌡 📍

Plenty of people grow blueberry for fruit. Why not for framework and fab fall color, too? Two species of the versatile berry thrive in the Northeast, and their names speak to size: highbush (*Vaccinium corymbosum*) and lowbush (*V. angustifolium*). The former makes the most common food crop, with a parade of cultivars in a variety of sizes. The latter, and smaller, boasts small edible berries too, and makes a great groundcover. All promise a fiery vision of fall, and all prefer acidic soil.

Highbush blueberry (*Vaccinium corymbosum* cultivar).

Viburnum species and cultivars

Viburnum

HARDINESS: Zones 2/3/4/5–9

BLOOM PERIOD: Midspring, late spring, early summer

SIZE: 3–12 ft. high, 3–15 ft. wide

D ☀ ◐ ◑ 🌡 📍

In the alphabet of the garden, it's a happy accident that "V" is for "versatile" as well as "viburnum." Few groups of shrubs do more or better. Plant one and see how your favorite feature changes through the seasons: flowers in spring or even winter, fruit late summer to fall, or fall foliage that dazzles most often in red-purple. Not convinced? How about crisp leaves throughout the growing season, and elegant form? It's tough to choose, with so many fantastic types, but here's a selection. Most viburnum grow 6–10 ft. tall and wide if left unpruned.

For berries, try *Viburnum dilatatum* 'Michael Dodge' (Zone 5) for yellow, American cranberry (*V. opulus* var. *americanum*, Zone 2) for red, or *V. dentatum* 'Blue Muffin' (Zone 3) for blue, a small shrub at 3–5 ft. For flower, it's tough to beat *V. sargentii* 'Onondaga' (Zone 4) for its flattened, circular blooms of red ringed with white. Snowball viburnum (*V. plicatum* f. *tomentosum*, Zone 4) is a close runner-up, with spheres of pure white among pleated leaves, as well as amazingly scented Korean spice viburnum (*V. carlesii*, Zone 4). Speaking of leaves, viburnum's more ornamental features often overshadow their fabulous foliage. Native cultivar *V. nudum* 'Winterthur' (Zone 5) is impeccably glossy, while big *V. rhytidophyllum* (Zone 5) is a semi-evergreen star with long leaves the texture of crocodile skin.

American cranberry viburnum (*Viburnum opulus* var. *americanum*). LEFT Snowball viburnum (*Viburnum plicatum* f. *tomentosum*). BELOW Korean spice viburnum (*Viburnum carlesii*).

Weigela florida cultivars

Weigela

HARDINESS: Zones 4–8

BLOOM PERIOD: Midspring, late spring, early summer

SIZE: 1–5 ft. high, 1–6 ft. wide

D ☀ 🌡

Pronounced "wy-JEE-luh", this shrub was once known for a seasonal show of spring flowers. Not so of modern weigela! Nowadays you'll find cultivars in various sizes, all of which do bloom prettily, but as an afterthought to bold, colorful foliage all throughout the growing seasons. 'Wine and Roses' dazzles with leaves of smoldering violet, while 'My Money' has green foliage edged in pink and white.

'Wine and Roses' weigela (*Weigela florida* 'Wine and Roses').

Xanthorhiza simplicissima

Yellowroot

HARDINESS: Zones 3–9

SIZE: 2–3 ft. high, 6 ft. or more wide

D ☀ ◐ ◑ ● ≡ 🌡 🦌 📍

An unsung groundcover begging for more use, yellowroot grows as a mat of glassy green, celery-like leaves, but there's more to this spreading shrub than meets the eye. It's an understated treasure with weird, wonderful purple chains of flowers in spring, and the purple returns in fall, with foliage that fades purple to gold. Plant this native in damp to moderately dry soil, even in shade.

Yellowroot (*Xanthorhiza simplicissima*).

Actaea species and cultivars

Baneberry, cohosh

HARDINESS: Zones 3–8

BLOOM PERIOD: Late spring, early summer, late summer, fall

SIZE: 2–6 ft. high, 2–3 ft. wide

H

Black cohosh (*Actaea simplex* cultivar).

Don't be put off by its foreboding common names. In the past, this group was known for flower, and while a few still fit the bill on that front, modern day *Actaea* cultivars excel for flashy, fine-textured foliage spanning three seasons. All prefer at least part shade, and make great additions to woodlands. 'Misty Blue' baneberry (*A. pachypoda* 'Misty Blue') is a native cultivar and a star in shade for its chilly blue foliage. Even better, it thrives in damp shade or dry. While white summer flowers are nothing of note, its berries (late summer to fall) will steal the show for sure: white with black dots, also called "doll's eyes." They're not for the eating, but for ornament, they're outstanding. Cultivars of black cohosh (*A. simplex*) also dazzle, as Goth garden accents. Look for the names 'Black Negligee', 'Brunette', and 'Hillside Black Beauty', references to their deep purple leaves. These plants prefer moist soil. In late summer, they'll also send up 6-ft. skyrockets of sweet pink-to-white flowers.

'Misty Blue' baneberry (*Actaea pachypoda* 'Misty Blue').

Ajuga reptans cultivars

Carpet bugle

HARDINESS: Zones 3–10

BLOOM PERIOD: Late spring, early summer

SIZE: 6–8 in. high, 12 in. or more wide

A "piece of cake" groundcover, carpet bugle spreads easily, and this tiny trooper's cultivars come in a palette of red, white, and purple. Carpet bugle's rosettes are evergreen unless they're buried in snow, and varieties bloom in late spring, in either blue or white. Beware its spreading tendencies if you don't like mixed lawn—if you do, it mingles well with lawn grasses, and makes an interesting contrast.

Carpet bugle (*Ajuga reptans* cultivar).

Alchemilla species

Lady's mantle

HARDINESS: Zones 3–8

BLOOM PERIOD: Early summer

SIZE: 1–2 ft. high, 1–3 ft. wide

Ever elegant in shade, this plant's shield-like leaves look soft, but shimmer with morning dew. Lady's mantle is a cinch in any soil with shade in the heat of the day, but plants take drier soils in shadier situations. Go with *Alchemilla mollis* if big leaves are your thing, or twee *A. alpina* for a teeny version of the same.

Lady's mantle (*Alchemilla mollis*).

Amsonia hubrichtii

Threadleaf bluestar

HARDINESS: Zones 5–8

BLOOM PERIOD: Midspring, late spring

SIZE: 2–3 ft. high and wide

A knee-high dome of fine-textured green, threadleaf bluestar is a trendy textural accent for fine foliage through the growing season. Like other bluestars, it blooms early summer, but its blue is near white. For those in search of fine texture but unimpressed by ornamental grasses, it makes an ideal alternative, and with a bonus: golden fall foliage, the best of its clan.

Threadleaf bluestar (*Amsonia hubrichtii*).

Aralia species and cultivars

Aralia

HARDINESS: Zones 3–9

BLOOM PERIOD: Midsummer, late summer

SIZE: 3–5 ft. high and wide

Aralia may be the most interesting plant you're not growing. Known by some as a prickly wild genus, some smaller cousins promise to make their way into more gardens. We're hard pressed for the tropical here where it's cold, and these two fit the bill in spades. Japanese *Aralia cordata* 'Sun King' makes for great all-season gold in light shade—best color will be with morning sun. It's even a vision in deeper shade, where its leaves turn to chartreuse. Its native counterpart, American spikenard (*A. racemosa*) also thrives in shady sites, blooms in sprays of summertime white, and tops it all off with bird-beloved purple berries into fall. It even takes moderate drought, or sun with moist soil. Since they die back each winter, big, bold aralias make great stand-ins for shrubs where winter cleanup is a must.

'Sun King' aralia (*Aralia cordata* 'Sun King').

Arctostaphylos uva-ursi and cultivars

Bearberry

HARDINESS: Zones 2–6

SIZE: 6–12 in. high, 3–6 ft. wide

Forever an underdog as a cold-climate groundcover, bearberry makes a tough mat in tiny circles of glossy green, like a carpet of boxwood, bejeweled in late summer by red berries that give it its common name. This Northeast native excels in average to dry soil in sun to part shade, and spreads well enough to cover ground, but slowly enough to keep in check. Same old groundcovers got you down? Give bearberry a try, and you'll soon be a convert.

Bearberry (*Arctostaphylos uva-ursi*).

Artemisia species and cultivars

Artemisia

HARDINESS: Zones 4–9

SIZE: 1–3 ft. high and wide

The first name in silver is artemisia for certain. Most elegant and least delicate, this group is the foam of the garden cappuccino. Aromatic artemisia loves growing in sun and loose soil, but any that's well drained will be to its liking. Sandy, salty seaside sites suit artemisia just fine, making it an atmospheric, multiseason addition to coastal gardens. Its pretty, scented leaves deter deer but can irritate skin in some people; best wear gloves when you prune. Speaking of pruning, artemisia's flowers are unsightly to some, but these can be sheared off if you find you're not a fan.

'Valerie Finnis' artemisia (*Artemisia ludoviciana* 'Valerie Finnis')

Artemisia schmidtiana 'Silver Mound' (Zone 3) and *A.* 'Powis Castle' (Zone 4) are classically lacy artemisias, with symmetrical leaves in sea foam shades of silver. The former stays low (1 ft. or less) and domelike, while the latter pushes rhizomes outward to form a clump more than 3 ft. Give 'Powis Castle' a haircut in early spring to keep it bushy. Unwanted flowers can be sheared off, too.

If you're in love with the color but would rather lose the lace, try cultivars of *Artemisia ludoviciana* 'Silver King' or 'Valerie Finnis'. These artemisias' leaves are wider than the others, and they spread to 3 ft., so give them some space.

'Silver Mound' artemisia (*Artemisia schmidtiana* 'Silver Mound').

Asarum species and cultivars

Wild ginger

HARDINESS: **Zones 4–8**

SIZE: **4–6 in. high, 6–12 in. wide**

If it's serious shine you're looking for in shade, European ginger (*Asarum europeaum*) seals the deal. This plant and its soft-leaved native cousin (*A. canadense*) make indestructible shade carpets in damp soil or dry. Both get their name from foliage that's ginger-scented when crushed, and unlike many groundcovers, they play politely with fellow perennials.

European ginger (*Asarum europaeum*).

Bergenia cordifolia cultivars

Bergenia

HARDINESS: Zones 3–8

BLOOM PERIOD: Late spring, early summer

SIZE: 1–2 ft. high and wide

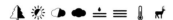

With its leathery, almost succulent leaves and multiseason appeal, bergenia works the garden like your best old garden gloves work the soil. Those leaves are a crisp, glossy green that shines in shade until temps cool, when they turn bronze. Tough bergenia prefers shade, damp soil or dry, and blooms in spring with primrose-like flowers from cultivars ranging from deep magenta to white. You can give winter-weary leaves and spent flower stalks a trim to keep it neat.

Bergenia (*Bergenia cordifolia*).

Brunnera cultivars

Brunnera

HARDINESS: Zones 3–7

BLOOM PERIOD: Late spring, early summer

SIZE: 18 in. high and wide

Brunnera makes a fat knot of bold multiseason foliage for shade, a great alternative to hosta if you find yourself tired of the latter. It thrives in average soil, but takes a bit of wet or dry, and color cultivars come in a piggy bank of metallic sheens: 'Looking Glass' in clear silver, 'Jack Frost' in silver spangles, and 'King's Ransom', edged in gold.

'Jack Frost' brunnera (*Brunnera macrophylla* 'Jack Frost').

Epimedium species and cultivars

Epimedium

HARDINESS: Zones 5–8

BLOOM PERIOD: Midspring, late spring

SIZE: 12–18 in. high and wide

By far one of the most popular stalwarts for shade, versatile epimedium has a world of other attributes: spring bloom; beautiful foliage all season long, some semi-evergreen; great potential as a groundcover. Give epimedium shade and dry to average soil, sit back, and discover your new favorite plant.

A large epimedium grown first for flower, cultivars of *Epimedium grandiflorum* create a rainbow in shade. Like other epimediums, its leaves are shaped like elongated hearts, but with this species, the leaves are punctuated by non-prickly spines. 'Lilafee' blooms lilac, 'Rose Queen' in mauve. Gardeners looking for foliage and flower to love should try *E. grandiflorum* var. *higoense* 'Bandit', a white-flowered form with leaves edged in maroon. Hybrid *E.* ×*rubrum* blooms pink and yellow, its leaves semi-evergreen, and it's often used as a spreading groundcover.

Two yellow-flowering hybrids are tough, semi-evergreen garden additions. Both 'Frohnleiten' and 'Sulphureum' are colorful groundcovers, stretching their legs to make a neat, leafy mat. The former blooms lemon yellow in spring, at the same time its new leaves appear with red marbling—a foliar treat that repeats with fall chill—and the latter is similar, but with flowers of a paler hue. 'Frohnleiten' may be the toughest epimedium of all, thriving in the deepest, driest shade you can throw at it.

***Epimedium* ×*rubrum*.** BELOW **'Sulphureum' epimedium (*Epimedium* 'Sulphureum').**

Euphorbia species and cultivars

Euphorbia, spurge

HARDINESS: Zones 4/5–8

BLOOM PERIOD: Late spring, early summer

SIZE: 1-3 ft. high, 1-2 ft. wide

They may not have the prettiest name, but these plants perform miracles when it comes to multiseason color and cover in tough spots. Easy and undemanding, euphorbias across the board require only a post-bloom trim to keep them neat and prompt a quick flush of new foliage. All require careful trimming, however, as the sap from their pretty leaves can irritate skin.

Cushion spurge (*Euphorbia polychroma*, Zone 4) is a euphorbia known for its sunny flowers, but it has skyrocketed to foliage stardom in cultivar 'Bonfire', a fire pit of crimson that contrasts with yellow-to-chartreuse spring bloom. 'First Blush' does the same, but with frosty white-edged foliage. Similar *E.* ×*martinii* 'Ascot Rainbow' (Zone 5) may promise the best show of all: rosettes with red centers and leaves edged decadently in gold, and yellow-green flowers with red eyes. All grow easily into neat domes of foliage, color best in sun, and prefer dry, well-drained soil.

If you've got shade to work with, try wood spurge (*Euphorbia amygdaloides* var. *robbiae*, Zone 4). Evergreen where snow isn't steep, its dark green rosettes are an excellent garden carpet in sun or shade, damp soil or dry, and in spring, this tiny dynamo sends up bunches of chartreuse blooms. Wood spurge may spread quickly in damp woodland soil, so give it room to do its thing.

'Bonfire' cushion spurge (*Euphorbia polychroma* 'Bonfire').

'Ascot Rainbow' euphorbia (*Euphorbia* ×*martinii* 'Ascot Rainbow').

Galium odoratum

Sweet woodruff

HARDINESS: Zones 4–8

BLOOM PERIOD: Midspring, late spring

SIZE: 6–12 in. high, 12–18 in. or more wide

Some of the best-scented plants are those whose fragrance is mysterious, and sweet woodruff is decidedly one of these. Crushed or dried foliage pipes a sweet perfume into the woodland air, but this tiny, starry groundcover could easily be missed. Sweet woodruff is easy in shade and not-too-dry soil.

Sweet woodruff (*Galium odoratum*).

Heuchera species and cultivars

Heuchera

HARDINESS: Zones 4–9

SIZE: 8 in.–3 ft. high, 1–2 ft. wide

H

If there's one foliage plant that came of age in the early twenty-first century, heuchera would be that plant, and for good reason: with a rainbow of color cultivars that thrive in all kinds of conditions, it's almost always a sure thing wherever it grows. You'll probably find dozens of heucheras at your local nursery, some for sun, and some shade. In the Northeast, most do best in part sun and well-drained soil of medium moisture—they'll take more sun in damp soil, and dry soil in shade. Plants with leaves of deeper hues need light to color well, but those with lighter leaves can be superstars in dry shade. Hybrids of *Heuchera villosa*, a mostly Southeast native whose range extends as far north as New York, will be happier where summers trend humid. A few popular cultivars include 'Caramel', with burnt orange foliage; 'Frosted Violet' which lives up to its name; 'Georgia Peach' in peachy red; and 'Dolce Key Lime' in chartreuse.

'Frosted Violet' heuchera (*Heuchera* 'Frosted Violet').

'Dolce Key Lime' heuchera (*Heuchera* 'Dolce Key Lime').

Hosta cultivars

Hosta

HARDINESS: Zones 3–9

SIZE: 1–4 ft. high, 1–5 ft. wide

H

Hosta is without a doubt one of the most popular plants today, and for good reason. Not only is it a piece of cake to grow, and a sure thing in shade, but with countless varieties in all kinds of shapes and colors, you're bound to find a hosta for you. Of the many hostas out there, all have a few things in common. Rich soil is best, and while hostas may handle dry shade, they'd much prefer damp. Speaking of shade, they'll be glad for part sun too—more in wet soil—but shade is always best in the hottest part of the day. Many gold varieties do well with morning sun to ensure their best color, and variegated varieties with whitest leaves will need it to grow.

When choosing a hosta, think about size first. Some grow into monsters, and some are tiny dynamos. (All grow more quickly in damp soil.) Color is the second consideration, and hostas come in an array, from cool blue to warm gold.

'Loyalist' hosta (*Hosta* 'Loyalist').

'Frances Williams' hosta (*Hosta sieboldiana* 'Frances Williams').

'Elegans' hosta (*Hosta sieboldiana* 'Elegans').

'Sum and Substance' hosta (*Hosta* 'Sum and Substance').

HOSTA CULTIVARS TO KNOW

Trying to make sense of hosta selection? Here are a few favorites based on color (mostly green, gold, blue, and white-variegated) and size (small—**S**, medium—**M**, and large—**L**).

MOSTLY GREEN	GOLD	BLUE	WHITE-VARIEGATED
'PRAYING HANDS' (S)	'RAINFOREST SUNRISE' (S)	'BLUE MOUSE EARS' (S)	'CHERRY BERRY' (S)
'AMERICAN SWEETHEART' (M)	'GUACAMOLE' (M)	'ABIQUA DRINKING GOURD' (M)	'LOYALIST' (M)
'SAGAE' (L)	'SUM AND SUBSTANCE' (L)	'ELEGANS' (L)	'GUARDIAN ANGEL' (L)

Macleaya cordata

Plume poppy

HARDINESS: Zones 3–8

BLOOM PERIOD: Late summer

SIZE: 5–8 ft. high, 2–6 ft. wide

Some big perennials can be treated like shrubs, and whopping plume poppy makes a great seasonal screen. With the right space to spread, it's a forest of silver leaves, towering up to 8 ft. and topped in clouds of summer salmon. Daring gardeners who are up to the task can try it with neighboring plants. Its spreading tendencies will lessen in shade and dry soil.

Plume poppy (*Macleaya cordata*).

Pachysandra species and cultivars

Pachysandra

HARDINESS: Zones 5–9

SIZE: 6–12 in. high, indefinite spread

Love it or hate it, Asian *Pachysandra terminalis* solves the problem of foolproof groundcover for dry shade—what most gardeners don't know is pachysandra need not be plain Jane. Cultivar 'Variegata' sports sea foam leaves edged in cream, while 'Green Sheen' glints with a million green mirrors. Even better, native *P. procumbens*, also called Allegheny spurge, has bigger, softer leaves, and fluffy white flowers. This last pachysandra spreads more modestly and prefers medium to moist soil.

'Silver Edge' pachysandra (*Pachysandra terminalis* 'Silver Edge').

Polemonium reptans cultivars

Jacob's ladder

HARDINESS: Zones 4–9

BLOOM PERIOD: Midspring, late spring

SIZE: 6–18 in. high, 12–18 in. wide

Variegated cultivars of native Jacob's ladder make stellar additions to shade gardens throughout the growing season. 'Stairway to Heaven' emerges in spring with green leaves thickly edged in pink, fading to white as the plant blooms in blue. Zebra-print 'Brise d'Anjou' does the same, but welcomes spring with creamy white. Both thrive in average conditions, and take moderately dry shade once established.

Variegated Jacob's ladder (*Polemonium reptans* 'Stairway to Heaven').

Polygonatum species and cultivars

Solomon's seal

HARDINESS: Zones 3/5–8

BLOOM PERIOD: Midspring, late spring

SIZE: 6–36 in. high, 1–3 ft. wide

Solomon's seal is an indispensable and surprisingly underused foliage plant for the shade garden. Its lilting, arcing stems exude a grace that belies this plant's toughness, as it thrives even in dry shade once it's settled in. Variegated Solomon's seal (*Polygonatum odoratum* 'Variegatum', Zone 3) boasts white-edged leaves and lights up the deepest of shady spots. A charming dwarf cousin, *P. humile* (Zone 5), glints with tiny leaves like green mirrors, and scarcely grows a foot tall.

Variegated Solomon's seal (*Polygonatum odoratum* 'Variegatum').

Rheum palmatum var. *tanguticum*, *R. rhabarbarum*

Rhubarb

HARDINESS: Zones 3–9

BLOOM PERIOD: Early summer, midsummer

SIZE: 3–6 ft. high, 4–6 ft. wide

H

If you love big, bold foliage but live in Montreal or Presque Isle, Maine, you're doing your garden a disservice in not growing rhubarb. This big perennial is a snap in sun and average to moist soil. Choose from the spiky, purely ornamental *Rheum palmatum* var. *tanguticum*, or the edible *R. rhabarbarum*, seldom planted in ornamental gardening. If you go with edible rhubarb, remember the stalks of the leaves are edible, but the leaves themselves are poisonous, and leave two-thirds of the plant to keep it going.

Ornamental rhubarb (*Rheum palmatum* var. *tanguticum*).

Rodgersia species and cultivars

Rodgersia

HARDINESS: Zones 5–7

BLOOM PERIOD: Midsummer

SIZE: 3–4 ft. high and wide

H

If you've got damp soil and enjoy exotic plants, rodgersia had better be on your radar. This wild, winged perennial adores wet soil and promises huge, palmlike leaves for those who hanker for warmer climes. In summer, it's topped off by cone-shaped froths of flower in white to pink. Rodgersia can handle average soil in shade, but damp is a must for sun.

Rodgersia (*Rodgersia* species).

Rubus pentalobus

Creeping raspberry

HARDINESS: Zones 6–9

SIZE: 4–6 in. high, indefinite spread

H

Creeping raspberry smothers weeds primly, with apple-green leaves you'll love but deer won't. These blush to bronze when temperatures drop. A raspberry grown for foliage, it thrives even in poor soil, and bubbles dramatically over edging and down walls.

Creeping raspberry (*Rubus pentalobus*).

Stachys byzantina and cultivars

Lamb's ear

HARDINESS: Zones 4–9

SIZE: 6–12 in. high, 12–24 in. wide

H

People don't often think of petting their plants, but you'll be hard pressed to resist lamb's ear. Each leaf of this gutsy groundcover is coated in the finest white down, and low-water lamb's ear brightens up any dull border. 'Helene von Stein', also called 'Big Ears', sports the largest leaves, and though lamb's ear loves sun, this cultivar will even take part shade.

'Helene von Stein' lamb's ear (*Stachys byzantina* 'Helene von Stein').

Thymus species and cultivars

Thyme

HARDINESS: Zones 4–9

BLOOM PERIOD: Early summer, midsummer

SIZE: 1–3 in. high, 1–2 ft. wide

If you grow thyme for cooking, try it for utility too. Varieties of this herb make a great groundcover and edging. For foot traffic, try creeping thyme (*Thymus serpyllum*) or cultivars of lemony *T. pulegioides*, which will perfume every footstep with their spicy scent. Silver-edge thyme (*T.* ×*citriodorus* 'Argenteus') looks smart as garden edging. All thymes adore bright light, heat, and dry soil, so they and your stepping stones will be a natural fit.

Thyme (*Thymus* species).

Tiarella species, hybrids, and cultivars

Foamflower

HARDINESS: Zones 4–9

BLOOM PERIOD: Early summer

SIZE: 6–18 in. high and wide

In need of a tough woodland groundcover for damp shade and dry? Foamflower is a native that makes an excellent semi-evergreen alternative to English ivy and vinca. Even better, this little plant blooms in spring, with white flowers held aloft on stems like tiny, flocked Christmas trees. Although foamflower is versatile, avoid planting it in wet soil.

Foamflower (*Tiarella* species).

Vinca minor and cultivars

Vinca

HARDINESS: Zones 4–8

BLOOM PERIOD: Late spring, early summer

SIZE: 4–6 in. high, indefinite spread

Though it may be much maligned, vinca is indubitably a bulletproof groundcover for even the toughest spots—especially shade. Take care to plant it where it has plenty of room to spread, but keep it from escaping into wild areas. Better yet, spice things up with a variegated cultivar, like golden 'Illumination'.

Vinca (*Vinca minor* cultivar).

Viola labradorica

Labrador violet

HARDINESS: Zones 3–8

BLOOM PERIOD: Late spring

SIZE: 4–6 in. high and wide

A little-used and amazing native groundcover, Labrador violet isn't a *Viola* for flower—it's a foliage plant. This little violet charms with deep purple leaves throughout the growing season, and spreads easily in sun to part shade and average soil. Like many groundcovers, Labrador violet spreads, seeding itself around and traveling by root, so best to give it some space.

Labrador violet (*Viola labradorica*).

FERNS

No group of plants is better loved for fine texture in shade than ferns, and these fine-feathered foliage plants are among the most dynamic in the plant kingdom. Though they may look delicate, ferns take more abuse than most any plant you'll find. Most love damp to medium soil—a few earn a spot in the dry shade design toolbox. All will ask for shade at least in the hottest part of the day.

Adiantum species

Maidenhair fern

HARDINESS: Zones 3/5–8

SIZE: 8–24 in. high and wide

H

Ferns personify fine texture, and maidenhair may be the finest-boned of all. Two types are worth noting: northern maidenhair (*Adiantum pedatum*) and Himalayan maidenhair fern (*A. venustum*). The former is a Northeast native, hardy to Zone 3, and has fronds that recall lacy green octopi. The latter is smaller, non-native, and grows in climates up to Zone 5. Its fronds are triangular. Both do best in average to moist soil, but will take moderately dry shade when well established.

Northern maidenhair fern (*Adiantum pedatum*).

Athyrium species, hybrids, and cultivars

Lady fern, painted fern

HARDINESS: Zones 4–9

SIZE: 2–3 ft. high and wide

H

Athyrium, or lady fern, may be the most popular genus among all ferns, and with good reason: these ladies know how to put on a show. While the native species most commonly called lady fern, *A. filix-femina*, promises the usual delicate fronds of green, its cousins are known for bolder, wilder colors. Japanese painted fern (*A. niponicum* var. *pictum*) shines in the shade with fronds of silver, while its cultivar 'Burgundy Lace' ups the ante in silvery pink. Hybrid 'Ghost' may be toughest of all, its leaves a lacy shade of mint, and thrives even in moderately dry shade. One variety of the native, 'Victoriae', does do these one better, its foliage like a fascinating green clump of foxtails. Similar to lady fern is hay-scented fern (*Dennstaedtia punctilobula*, Zone 3), another native that spreads to form colonies and takes moderately dry shade once established.

Lady fern (*Athyrium filix-femina*). BELOW 'Ghost' fern (*Athyrium* 'Ghost').

Dryopteris erythrosora and cultivars

Autumn fern

HARDINESS: Zones 5–9

SIZE: 1–3 ft. high and wide

In spite of its name, autumn fern isn't just for fall interest, and in fact is most interesting the first half of the growing season. It gets its name from new fronds the color of orange fall leaves—these age to a deep hunter green as the season wears on. Cultivar 'Brilliance' is said to emerge brighter, and keep its color longer.

Autumn fern (*Dryopteris erythrosora*).

Matteuccia struthiopteris

Ostrich fern

HARDINESS: Zones 3–8

SIZE: 2–3 ft. high and wide

H

The first name in form in the world of ferns, ostrich fern makes a simple yet spectacular display. In spring, its fiddlehead plumage unfurls into a symmetrical, circular crown, each green frond reminiscent of a feather of that giant bird. Ostrich fern thrives in average to wet soil, especially on damp sites. Its early spring fiddleheads are edible as well.

Ostrich fern (*Matteuccia struthiopteris*).

Osmunda cinnamomea, O. regalis

Cinnamon fern and royal fern

HARDINESS: Zones 3–9

SIZE: 2–3 ft. high and wide

H

While most ferns bear seeds (called spores) underneath their green leaves, these two ferns of distinction sprout central topknots of fertile fronds just for that purpose. Cinnamon fern (*Osmunda cinnamomea*) gets its name from this funky foliage, so bulky and brown it resembles cinnamon sticks. Royal fern (*O. regalis*) is bolder in texture, and its fertile leaves look more like tassels. Both thrive on wet sites, but also adapt to average soils.

Cinnamon fern (*Osmunda cinnamomea*).

Polystichum acrostichoides, P. polyblepharum

Christmas fern, tassel fern

HARDINESS: **Zones 3/5–9**

SIZE: **2–3 ft. high and wide**

Some of the easiest and most ornamental ferns fall into the genus *Polystichum*. Zone 3–hardy Christmas fern (*P. acrostichoides*) gets its name from semi-evergreen foliage that sticks around well into winter, if it's not flattened by heavy snow. This native beauty boasts long, sword-shaped fronds, thrives in dry shade, and clumps up to make a fab, refined groundcover. Asian cousin tassel fern (*P. polyblepharum*) promises intricate rosettes of ultra-glossy leaves. Cold-hardy to Zone 5, it proves semi-evergreen as well.

Christmas fern (*Polystichum acrostichoides*).

GRASSES

Forget those mouse-brown ornamental grasses of yesteryear—today's garden grasses make up one of the most visually dynamic families of plants available, unrivaled as textural elements for multiseason interest. Whether it's sun or shade, wet soil or dry, there's bound to be a grass that's right for your garden. Grasses typically come in two types: cool-season versions that do most of their growing in spring and fall; and warm-season, which begin to grow most when temps warm in late spring.

Calamagrostis ×acutiflora cultivars

Feather reed grass

HARDINESS: **Zones 5–9**

BLOOM PERIOD: **Late spring, early summer**

SIZE: **4–6 ft. high, 2–3 ft. wide**

H ☀ ☀ ◑ ≡ 🦌

These cool-season grasses serve as season-long showstoppers. They appear early, leafing out in spring, then send up a sheer column of plumes that open in shades of pink. If that weren't enough, these fade and dry by midsummer, making a bicolor green and white pillar perfect as a vertical accent. 'Karl Foerster' is most popular, with white-edged 'Overdam' a close second. Adaptable feather reed grasses even thrive in light shade.

'Karl Foerster' feather reed grass (*Calamagrostis ×acutiflora* 'Karl Foerster').

Carex species and cultivars

Sedge

HARDINESS: Zones 3/4/5–9

SIZE: 8 in.–3 ft. tall, 1–3 ft. wide

D

Sedges aren't technically grasses, but they're visually similar, so they're included here for our purposes. Beyond their similarity to grasses, sedges are a many and varied group, and come in a variety of shapes and sizes, not to mention colors. In Zone 5–hardy, fine-textured sedges, there's red-orange *Carex buchananii*, yellow *C. oshimensis* 'Evergold', blue *C. flacca* 'Blue Zinger', and many greens, like native lawn alternative Pennsylvania sedge (*C. pensylvanica*, Zone 3). All these sedges thrive in part sun to part shade. For a bolder statement in sun, try golden palm sedge (*C. muskingumensis* 'Oehme', Zone 4), or white-striped *C. siderosticha* 'Variegata' (Zone 5) for shade. Most sedges do well in average to moist soil, but take moderately dry soil once established.

Pennsylvania sedge (*Carex pensylvanica*). BELOW 'Oehme' palm sedge (*Carex muskingumensis* 'Oehme').

Chasmanthium latifolium and cultivars

River oats

HARDINESS: Zones 3–8

BLOOM PERIOD: Late summer

SIZE: 2–5 ft. high, 1–2 ft. wide

Tall grasses for shade can be a tall order. Enter river oats, an ethereal native grass that takes shade in spades. River oats makes cane-like stalks that resemble bamboo, and in summer, its odd flowers appear, each like a flattened fishtail that ages to brown. This grass will seed around happily in wet soil—planting in dry shade helps keep it in check. Cultivar 'River Mist' brightens shady spaces with boldly white-edged leaves.

River oats (*Chasmanthium latifolium*).

Deschampsia species and cultivars

Hair grass

HARDINESS: Zones 4–9

BLOOM PERIOD: Midsummer, late summer

SIZE: 1–3 ft. high, 1–2 ft. wide

Underused in the world of grasses, tufted hair grass (*Deschampsia cespitosa*) and crinkled hair grass (*D. flexuosa*) make neat, spherical clumps of green, and send up apple-green flowers in early summer. These plumes age to an oaten color, and make a perfect foil for foliage until fall. Cool-season hair grasses are native to temperate regions worldwide, and thrive even in part shade. Sunny cultivar 'Tatra Gold' has yellow-green leaves that turn burnished in fall.

'Tatra Gold' hair grass (*Deschampsia flexuosa* 'Tatra Gold').
RIGHT Blue fescue (*Festuca glauca*).

Festuca glauca and cultivars

Blue fescue

HARDINESS: Zones 4–8

SIZE: 2–5 ft. high, 1–2 ft. wide

Blue fescue makes a neat, steely globe and excels in full sun and rocky, sandy soil, the perfect thing to bring some bling to the toughest spots in your yard. A semi-evergreen grass, its foliage should be sheared back in late winter, before a new flush emerges. For even bluer foliage, try cultivar 'Elijah Blue'. This grass is sometimes called *Festuca ovina glauca*.

Hakonechloa macra and cultivars

Japanese forest grass

HARDINESS: Zones 5–9

SIZE: 1–3 ft. high and wide

Ever wanted bamboo, but don't have the space? Each clump of Japanese forest grass looks like a whole grove of bamboo in miniature, and this shade-loving grass doesn't spread in the least—a treat for small gardens in search of Asian accents. Moreover, Japanese forest grass is one tough cookie, adapting readily to moderately dry shade and dazzling with cultivars like yellow-lined 'Aureola' and white-edged 'Fubuki'. 'Beni-Kaze' and 'Nicolas' bring amazing red fall color to shady spaces.

Liriope species and cultivars, *Ophiopogon* species and cultivars

Lilyturf, mondo grass

HARDINESS: Zones 4/5/6–10

BLOOM PERIOD: Late summer

SIZE: 2–24 in. high, 4–24 in. wide

Though not technically grasses and two different species, these plants often get lumped together, and with grasses, because they're so similar in many ways. Both make superb, slowly spreading groundcovers, thick enough to choke weeds. Their grassy leaves are evergreen (a rarity among grasses and allies in the Northeast), although they tend to look worse for wear after winter. If they've browned, give them a haircut before spring. *Liriope spicata* spreads fastest, and is hardy to Zone 4. For bigger and beefier, consider a cultivar of cousin *L. muscari* called 'Big Blue' (Zone 5); for smaller and more fine-textured, go with *Ophiopogon japonicus* 'Nana' (Zone 6). Of course, black plant enthusiasts can't resist black mondo grass (*O. planiscapus* 'Nigrescens', Zone 6).

Japanese forest grass (*Hakonechloa macra*).
RIGHT Black mondo grass (*Ophiopogon planiscapus* 'Nigrescens').

Miscanthus sinensis cultivars

Miscanthus

HARDINESS: **Zones 5/6–9**

BLOOM PERIOD: **Fall**

SIZE: **1–8 ft. high, 1–6 ft. wide**

H ☀ ◐ 🦌

Definitely the most popular ornamental grass on the market, miscanthus is more known by its botanical name these days than its common ("maiden grass"). An easy-to-grow grass in sun and most any soil, miscanthus comes in a menagerie of cultivars for color and texture. Love variegated leaves? Try broad-leaved 'Cosmopolitan' (Zone 6), with circus tent stripes of white, or spiky zebra grass ('Zebrinus', Zone 5), gold-banded and bamboo-like. For Zone 5-hardy fine texture, 'Gracillimus' is second only to 'Morning Light', which adds silvery foliage. All these grow 6–8 ft. Smaller varieties include 'Gold Bar', a mini-'Zebrinus' at 5 ft., and frisky 'Little Kitten' at 3 ft., both hardy to Zone 5. Miscanthus should be cut to the ground in late winter.

Zebra grass (*Miscanthus sinensis* 'Zebrinus') BELOW 'Morning Light' miscanthus (*Miscanthus sinensis* 'Morning Light').

Panicum virgatum and cultivars

Switch grass

HARDINESS: Zones 5–9

BLOOM PERIOD: Late summer, fall

SIZE: 4–6 ft. high, 2–5 ft. wide

H

One of the great success stories in grass and native plants, too, nearly a dozen fabulous switch grass cultivars have exploded onto the market in the past ten years. A sure thing in sun and lean, dry soil, this warm-season grass may get floppy in too much water or shade—that said, they make a terrific accent draped at the edge of a pond. 'Northwind' wins out with vertical swords of blue-gray, a perfect columnar accent. 'Dallas Blues' may be bluest, and also blooms pink, while 'Ruby Ribbons' and 'Prairie Fire' blush to shades of wine mid-season.

'Dallas Blues' switch grass (*Panicum virgatum* 'Dallas Blues').
BELOW 'Prairie Fire' switch grass (*Panicum virgatum* 'Prairie Fire').

Pennisetum alopecuroides cultivars

Fountain grass

HARDINESS: Zones 5–9

BLOOM PERIOD: Late summer, fall

SIZE: 2–3 ft. high, 1–2 ft. wide

H ☀ ≡ 🦌

A classic among ornamental grasses, fountain grass grows as a tidy, fine-textured green globe until long drumstick plumes at the end of longer stems poke their heads out from its center late in the season. 'Hameln' and smaller 'Little Bunny' are finest, and their brown sugar–colored flowers are natural accents for fall. Bigger, more colorful cultivars like black-plumed 'Moudry' and cinnamon 'Red Head' (a midsummer bloomer) make a more substantial statement. Sun is a must for fountain grasses.

'Little Bunny' fountain grass (*Pennisetum alopecuroides* 'Little Bunny').

Pennisetum orientale and cultivars

Oriental fountain grass

HARDINESS: Zones 6–9

BLOOM PERIOD: Midsummer, late summer, fall

SIZE: 3–4 ft. high and wide

H ☀ ◐ ≡ 🦌

Fuzzy flowers of Oriental fountain grass are a sure sign summer is here, and this grass blooms straight on until frost. The species blooms white, along with upright cultivar 'Tall Tails', while superstar 'Karley Rose' flowers in dusky pink. Don't be fooled by its modest footprint when cut back in late winter—this is a big grass that spreads out to around twice that circumference, and easily smothers weeds in its path. Like other fountain grasses, it thrives in sun and flops in shade.

'Karley Rose' oriental fountain grass (*Pennisetum orientale* 'Karley Rose').

SUCCULENTS

A dynamic and determined group of garden stalwarts, succulents have enjoyed a well-deserved surge in garden popularity. Hardy succulents in the Northeast face special challenges, thanks to our below-freezing winters and high-humidity summers—conditions succulents tend to dislike—but a few earn a worthy place in many a northeastern garden. Succulents thrive in difficult conditions: blazing sun, salt spray, and lean, mean, sandy or rocky soil.

Opuntia humifusa

Eastern prickly pear

HARDINESS: Zones 4–10

BLOOM PERIOD: Early summer

SIZE: 8–14 in. high, 12–18 in. wide

When you think of cold climate gardens, cacti probably aren't the first plant that come to mind, but eastern prickly pear is a cactus that calls the Northeast home. This lively little plant blooms with glowing, buttery, bowl-shaped flowers in summer, and makes a bold foliage accent all through the growing season. Though nearly spineless, tiny prickers called glochids mean it should still be handled with kid gloves—or, better yet, dish gloves.

Eastern prickly pear (*Opuntia humifusa*).

Sedum species and cultivars

Creeping sedum

HARDINESS: Zones 3–9

BLOOM PERIOD: Late summer, fall

SIZE: 1–3 in. high, indefinite spread

H ☀ ◐ ≡ 🌡 🦌

Proving great things can come in small packages, creeping sedum makes an exquisite groundcover for sun and lean soil, in a rainbow of colors to suit any discerning gardener. Citron *Sedum rupestre* 'Angelina' spreads quickly and blooms gold, while cool *S. reflexum* 'Blue Spruce' flowers pink. *S. spurium* 'Dragon's Blood' features red flowers and reddish leaves; 'Bertram Anderson' brings purple foliage and fuchsia flower. A tiny non-spreader worth trying is October daphne (*S. sieboldii*), with turquoise foliage and pink flower.

'Angelina' sedum (*Sedum rupestre* 'Angelina').

Sedum spectabile cultivars, *S. telephium* cultivars

Stonecrop

HARDINESS: Zones 3–9

BLOOM PERIOD: Late summer, fall

SIZE: 2–3 ft. high and wide

H ☀ ◐ ≡ 🌡 🦌

A tall, clumping first cousin of low-growing sedum, stonecrop illustrates the sheer diversity of plants in the succulent genre. This fleshy perennial erupts from rosettes in early spring and spends the growing season inching ever skyward until late summer, when bouquets of tiny flowers appear at the end of its long stems. These open over a long period before turning a wheaten color in winter for interest until heavy snow arrives. Favorite 'Matrona' bears wine-colored stems and rosy blooms, while 'Autumn Joy' and 'Autumn Fire' flower red. Stonecrops may flop in shade or rich soil. Their genus is sometimes listed as *Hylotelephium*.

'Matrona' sedum (*Sedum telephium* 'Matrona').

Sempervivum tectorum and cultivars

Sempervivum

HARDINESS: Zones 3–8

SIZE: 1–3 in. high, 6–18 in. wide

Also called "live forever," this tiny succulent lives up to its name, thriving in cracks and crannies no other plants could. Each one a symmetrical, geometrical rosette of fleshy, often vividly colored leaves, sempervivums make ideal subjects for filling in sunny terraces and walls.

Sempervivum (*Sempervivum tectorum*).

Yucca species and cultivars

Yucca

HARDINESS: Zones 5–10

BLOOM PERIOD: Midsummer

SIZE: 2–4 ft. high (6-8 ft. in flower); 2–3 ft. wide

Common green yucca (*Yucca filamentosa*) fell out of favor in gardens when it became a favorite for parking lots, and this is a shame, because for architectural texture, yucca can't be beat. Luckily, new, more colorful cultivars are courting gardeners today, like golden 'Color Guard' and gilt-glazed 'Bright Edge'. If it's cool colors you're craving, try *Y. rostrata* 'Sapphire Skies', a tropicalesque stunner that even grows a trunk with age.

'Color Guard' yucca (*Yucca filamentosa* 'Color Guard').

SPRING

Early Risers That Shine

As we discussed earlier, spring is perhaps the most restless of seasons in the landscape of the Northeast. One day a warm spell has us venturing hesitantly outdoors after winter's hibernation—the next sees us fleeing a plunge back to freezing. Spring in the Northeast is the test of our fearlessness as gardeners. Luckily, spring plants have evolved to be a fearless bunch, too.

TREES, SHRUBS, AND VINES

Amelanchier species and cultivars

Shadblow

HARDINESS: Zones 4–9

BLOOM PERIOD: Midspring

SIZE: 15–25 ft. high and wide

D

Ever recommended yet somehow rarely planted, this polite, small tree greets spring with billows of white, a precursor to blue berries for you and the birds. Shadblow's fall plumage is fantastic red or orange—more so in cultivars like 'Autumn Brilliance'—and its size makes it an ideal small tree or large shrub for many landscapes. Cultivar 'Robin Hill' blooms pink. Species *Amelanchier arborea*, *A. canadensis*, and *A. laevis* are just a few native to the Northeast.

Camassia (*Camassia*) blooming against a background of 'Ogon' dawn redwood (*Metasequoia glyptostroboides* 'Ogon').

Shadblow (*Amelanchier* species).

Cercis canadensis and cultivars

Redbud

HARDINESS: Zones 4–9

BLOOM PERIOD: Midspring

SIZE: 20–30 ft. high, 25–35 ft. wide

D

Northeast native redbud forever stands in the shadow of that other showy spring-flowering tree, dogwood, but this stalwart deserves much more garden attention. Adaptable redbud excels even in dry sites, sun or part shade, and blushes with spring blooms in pink to lavender. Its heart-shaped foliage makes it spiffy throughout the growing season, turning a pretty yellow in fall. For an even longer season of interest, try purple-leaved 'Forest Pansy' or gleaming 'Hearts of Gold'.

Redbud (*Cercis canadensis*).

Chaenomeles species and cultivars

Flowering quince

HARDINESS: Zones 4/5–8

BLOOM PERIOD: Early spring, midspring

SIZE: 4–10 ft. high and wide

D

Take a break from the delicate pastels of spring with flowering quince, a tough shrub that smothers itself in hot coral or crimson before it leafs out. Flowering quince makes an ideal loose hedge, and tackles drought with no problem once it's established. Cultivars of *Chaenomeles* ×*superba*, including those listed here, are generally considered hardy to Zone 4, while those of *C. speciosa* winter up to Zone 5. *C.* ×*superba* 'Texas Scarlet' is an old-fashioned, thorny favorite, while thornless newcomers in the Storm series (cultivars of *C. speciosa*) bloom with more ruffly flowers of red, orange, and pink. For those who still yearn for quieter hues, *C.* ×*superba* 'Cameo' blooms in softest peach, and *C. speciosa* 'Toyo-Nishiki' and 'O Yashima' in cascades of pink and white, respectively.

Flowering quince (*Chaenomeles* cultivar).

Cornus species and cultivars

Dogwood

HARDINESS: **Zones 3/5–9**

BLOOM PERIOD: **Midspring, late spring, early summer**

SIZE: **15–30 ft. high and wide**

D

Known the world over for fabulous flower early in the growing season, many dogwoods are lookers even beyond spring. As a rule, all would prefer soil that isn't too wet or dry, and as understory trees, shade in at least the heat of the day.

Native flowering dogwood (*Cornus florida*, Zone 5) blooms in gentle white or pink above nude branches before leafing out. An easy plant when conditions are right, it won't stand for hot sites, soggy or sere soil. Give it good, cool ground, a bit of shade, and you'll be rewarded not just with that, but fiery red fall color. Poorly sited plants inevitably attract dogwood anthracnose, a fungal pest. Consider other species if anthracnose is diagnosed in your neighborhood. Kousa dogwood (*C. kousa*, Zone 5), its Asian counterpart, is one. Kousa blooms later, but arguably greater—its striking flowers in white or pink appear in a whitewater flood of spring bloom as a follow-up to glossy leaves. In summer, it serves up a sea of circular red berries, a treat for birds, and fall foliage of red to purple. Kousa dogwood adapts better to sun and periods of dry weather.

Another native dogwood is hardier and has a Far East flair. Pagoda dogwood (*Cornus alternifolia*, Zone 3) is so named for tiers of structurally splendid branches. This small tree (15–25 ft.) bursts forth with fuzzy powderpuffs of creamy flowers in spring, followed by vibrant red and blue berries birds adore, and finishing with autumn "in the red" for multiseason interest. A versatile tree happy with some shade, give it soil on the damp side in hot, sunny sites.

Flowering dogwood (*Cornus florida*).

Kousa dogwood (*Cornus kousa*).

Daphne species and cultivars

Daphne

HARDINESS: Zones 4–8

BLOOM PERIOD: Late spring

SIZE: 2–4 ft. high and wide

D

Fragrant-flowered daphne can be a fickle mistress, but she's well worth it with a little careful planning. Plant daphne in sun and soil with good drainage, especially in winter—soggy soil for daphne simply won't do. Plant it in a place it can live long-term, and avoid pruning, as all of these factors are thought to contribute to mysterious "daphne death," a still-unexplained phenomenon in the gardening world. *Daphne* ×*burkwoodii* 'Carol Mackie' is popular, with pink-white flowers fluttering above variegated foliage. Purple *D. mezereum* blooms earliest, following up with pretty, poisonous red fruit in summer.

'Carol Mackie' daphne (*Daphne* ×*burkwoodii* 'Carol Mackie').

Enkianthus campanulatus and cultivars

Enkianthus

HARDINESS: Zones 4–8

BLOOM PERIOD: Late spring, early summer

SIZE: 6–10 ft. high, 4–6 ft. wide

D

A long-blooming, hot-colored harbinger of summer, enkianthus's tiny bells cap off the spring flowering season. A quietly architectural shrub, its upright form makes a statement year-round, and underused enkianthus shows off again with red foliage in fall. Two popular cultivars are 'Showy Lantern' and 'Red Bells'. White-flowering varieties are available as well.

Enkianthus (*Enkianthus campanulatus*).

Forsythia species and cultivars

Forsythia

HARDINESS: Zones 5–8

BLOOM PERIOD: Early spring, midspring

SIZE: 8–10 ft. high, 10–12 ft. wide

D

Many are wooed by forsythia's gilded spring display, and indeed, its galloping sprays of gold flowers are a welcome turn from dark winter months. Forsythia makes a simple, long-lived, no-maintenance shrub if you remember two things. First, it's big and informal. Give it plenty of room to grow, and don't try to shear it into a box. Second, it fades into the background post-bloom, so group it with other plants to take up the torch the rest of the year.

Forsythia (*Forsythia* species).

Halesia carolina

Carolina silverbell

HARDINESS: Zones 4–8

BLOOM PERIOD: Midspring

SIZE: 30–40 ft. high, 20–30 ft. wide

D ☀ ☀ ◑ ≡ 🌡

A vision in thousands of dangly white blooms, this is one southern belle that lives up to its name. Silverbell is striking in spring flower, before it leafs out—after that, its medium-large leaves make it a bit more boldly textured through the course of the season, and this foliage also turns a modest gold in fall. Silverbell is easy in sun to part shade and average soil. It's sometimes called *Halesia tetraptera*.

Carolina silverbell (*Halesia carolina*).

Kolkwitzia amabilis and cultivars

Beauty bush

HARDINESS: Zones 4–8

BLOOM PERIOD: Midspring, late spring

SIZE: 6–10 ft. high and wide

D ☀ ☀ ◑ ≡ 🌡 🦌

A simple, old-fashioned shrub underused in landscapes today, beauty bush billows with bubblegum-scented pink flowers in late spring. This drought-resistant darling gets big and tall with age, its vase shape alluring, its exfoliating bark a woody accent. For best shape, prune after blooming, and keep suckers in check. Cultivar 'Dream Catcher' does all this with raucous gold foliage. It grows best with afternoon shade to guard against scorching.

'Dream Catcher' beauty bush (*Kolkwitzia amabilis* 'Dream Catcher').

Magnolia species and cultivars

Magnolia, spring-flowering

HARDINESS: Zones 4/5/6–9

BLOOM PERIOD: Early spring, midspring, late spring, early summer

SIZE: 10–35 ft. high, 8–30 ft. wide

D

Early-flowering magnolias are among the first flowery heralds of winter's end, and with Northeasterners' enthusiasm for plants that signal spring, lots of species and cultivars can be found at your local nursery. Above all, most grow easily in soil of average moisture in full sun to part shade, but mags appreciate some shade in the heat of the day. Late snow and frost are magnolia lovers' greatest fear, but opting for a later bloomer or careful siting of

Saucer magnolia (*Magnolia* ×*soulangeana*).

an early one can be the difference between fresh or foul magnolia flowers.

Saucer magnolia (*Magnolia* ×*soulangeana* cultivars, Zone 4) blooms early, and for the winter-weary gardener, it's a sight for dinner plate–sized sore eyes. Porcelain flowers polka dot this tree's bare branches, each in gradations of lavender to pink to white. Saucers are often casualties to unpredictable chills during spring in the Northeast—plant them in a spot that's more shaded this time of year, and you can often put bloom off just long enough to escape a late freeze.

Two yellow-flowering hybrids, 'Elizabeth' and 'Butterflies' (Zone 5), get their buttery color from a shared parent: cucumber tree (*Magnolia acuminata*). More importantly, these fragrant beauties inherited that parent's tendency to bloom later in spring, so their delicate-but-dazzling floral display is less likely damaged by late frost. 'Elizabeth' grows a bit larger, topping out at 30 feet, while 'Butterflies' tends toward 20. Later still is Oyama magnolia (*M. sieboldii*, Zone 6), with gigantic foot-long leaves, a bold foliar accent akin to more southerly climes. It wows in late spring with huge tricolor blooms: white on the outside, pink/red and yellow in the center.

'Butterflies' magnolia (*Magnolia* 'Butterflies').

Malus cultivars

Flowering crabapple

HARDINESS: Zones 4–8

BLOOM PERIOD: Midspring

SIZE: 15–25 ft. high and wide

Fruit trees can be magnets for pests and diseases, ornamentals included. Fortunately for flowering crabapples, many modern cultivars resist pests and diseases better than their predecessors. Flowering crabs roll out the red carpet for their show in spring—or the pink or white carpet, if we're talking flower color. 'Prairiefire' is a popular plant for its dusky bubblegum pink, a precursor to red fruit the rest of the season. 'Holiday Gold' blooms white, then loads up with golden pomes, while at 5 ft., tiny 'Tina' trades white flowers for red fruit later on. 'Jackii' crab's white display may barely rival its red-orange fall leaves, a spectacular sight coupled with crabapples of red.

Flowering crabapple (*Malus* cultivar).

Pieris japonica and cultivars

Pieris

HARDINESS: Zones 5–8

BLOOM PERIOD: Early spring, midspring

SIZE: 4–12 ft. high, 3–8 ft. wide

Exciting cultivars of this deer-resistant favorite make pieris worth a second look. The common thread between varieties of this rhodie relative is their cascade of early spring flower, followed closely by colorful, contrasting new foliage, most in shades of red. Cabernet-colored spring leaves makes 'Katsura' a star, while variegated 'Flaming Silver' flashes fire engine–red above white-edged green foliage of green. 'Dorothy Wyckoff' blooms begin almost purple, and mature through pastel pink to white. Variegated 'Little Heath', a tiny gem at 3–4 ft., looks dusted in silver year-round.

Pieris (*Pieris japonica* cultivar).

Prunus species and cultivars

Ornamental cherry and plum

HARDINESS: Zones 2/4/5–8

BLOOM PERIOD: Early spring, midspring

SIZE: 6–35 ft. high, 5–30 ft. wide

D ☀ ◐ 🌡

Not all fruit is for the eating, and spring finds ornamental cherry and plum at their peak. Longevity is the watchword for ornamental cherry, and two popular trees that have proven more enduring in gardens are higan cherry (*Prunus subhirtella* 'Autumnalis', Zone 4) and Sargent cherry (*P. sargentii*, Zone 5). Higan bursts with spring petticoats of pink-white and also comes in a popular weeping form, 'Pendula'. Sargent flowers in an array of pinks, with burnished red-orange bark for good measure. For a more shrubby spring cherry, try purple-leaf sand cherry (*P.* ×*cistena*), a Zone 2–hardy pink bloomer at 6 ft. with wild purple foliage through the growing season. Two plums also sizzle with purple foliage: *P. cerasifera* 'Thundercloud' (Zone 5) and 'Newport' (Zone 4). All thrive in sun and average to moist, well-drained soil, and though they are attractive to hungry pests and diseases, their spring show is worth the risk to many a fearless gardener.

Sargent cherry (*Prunus sargentii*).

Rhododendron species and cultivars

Rhododendron

HARDINESS: Zones 4/5/6–9

BLOOM PERIOD: Early spring, midspring, late spring, early summer

SIZE: 2–15 ft. high and wide

Second to lilac, rhododendron may be the most beloved flowering shrub in our region. This many and varied genus comes in an arsenal of cultivars in color and texture for gardens of all kinds, from deciduous and small-leaved azaleas to evergreen leviathans. Many are old fashioned, overused and abused, but an

'Wojnar's Purple' rhododendron (*Rhododendron* 'Wojnar's Purple').

'Gibraltar' Exbury azalea (*Rhododendron* 'Gibraltar').

'Ken Janeck' rhododendron (*Rhododendron yakushimanum* 'Ken Janeck').

equally many are underrated and awaiting their star turn. All thrive in rich, well-drained, acidic soil. In the cool Northeast, rhodies tolerate more sun, but they thrive in the high, bright shade of tall trees. The rhododendrons included here are a small selection of the many stalwarts and underdogs deserving of more use in this genus.

'Blue Baron' (Zone 5) is a small blue wonder, while 'Wojnar's Purple' (Zone 5) makes a bigger splash from that side of the color wheel. *Rhododendron prinophyllum* 'Marie Hoffman' (Zone 5), 'Compacta' Korean azalea (*R. yedoense* var. *poukhanense* 'Compacta', Zone 4), and 'Olga Mezitt' (Zone 4) are all dazzlers in bright pink. 'Capistrano' (Zone 5) is a rare pale yellow, and subtle hints of yellow mix deliciously with pink in *R. yakushimanum* cultivars 'Ken Janeck' (Zone 5) and 'Percy Wiseman' (Zone 6). Nothing subtle about 'Gibraltar' (Zone 5), on the other hand, an orange-flowered azalea that's the focal point of any color combo. Looking for rhodie bloom later in the growing season? Try native rosebay (*R. maximum*, Zone 4), a pink-flowering giant at 8–15 ft.

Syringa species and cultivars

Lilac

HARDINESS: Zones 4–8

BLOOM PERIOD: Midspring, late spring, early summer

SIZE: 4–15 ft. high, 5–12 ft. wide

D

What would spring in the Northeast be without lilac? This clan of blousy bloomers struts its stuff with fragrant flowers early in the season, and lilac happens to be happiest in our part of the country. Lilac thrives in full sun and good air circulation—shaded plants quickly get leggy, and humidity promotes powdery mildew. Lilacs like to sucker, so have pruners at the ready.

'Palibin' dwarf lilac (*Syringa meyeri* 'Palibin').

Common lilac (*Syringa vulgaris*) is everyone's favorite flower in the glorious Northeast spring, and its sweetly scented bushels of bloom make it a top spring seasonal in your garden and indoors, as a cut flower. Favorite cultivars include pink 'Maiden's Blush', blue 'President Grevy', creamy 'Primrose', purple 'Henri Robert', and white-edged purple 'Sensation'. Earlier-blooming varieties of similar *S. hyacinthaflora* kick off the season, including purple 'Asessippi'.

Two small lilacs make up in flower power and disease-resistance what they may lack in size: *Syringa meyeri* 'Palibin' and *S. pubescens* subsp. *patula* 'Miss Kim'. At around 5 ft., these lilacs delight gardeners even in small spaces. Both bloom in shades of lavender, a bit later than their big cousins. A rare lilac to grow for foliage and flower, 'Palibin' rounds out the season with tidy, teeny rounded leaves. On the other end of the size spectrum, tree lilac (*S. reticulata*, Zone 3) promises fragrant, creamy flowers in summer, the perfect contrast to dark green, disease-resistant leaves. It makes an excellent small accent tree for lawn or by street, and its cherry-like bark makes it a beauty year-round.

'Sensation' lilac (*Syringa vulgaris* 'Sensation').

Wisteria species

Wisteria

HARDINESS: Zones 5–9

BLOOM PERIOD: Late spring, early summer

SIZE: 15–30 ft. high, 4–8 ft. wide

D ☀ ◐ ≡ 🦌 📍

Legendary for its purple chains of spring flower, Chinese wisteria (*Wisteria sinensis*) has been a garden mainstay for decades—even if many a gardener finds themselves woefully unprepared for its scale at maturity. The classic wisteria needs regular pruning once it grows up, and close attention to make sure it doesn't spread to wild places. If you're concerned this wily vine may fly the coop, native American wisteria (*W. frutescens*) is a safer choice, and flowers earlier.

American wisteria (*Wisteria frutescens*).

Chinese wisteria (*Wisteria sinensis*).

PERENNIALS, BULBS, AND ANNUALS

Aquilegia species and cultivars

Columbine

HARDINESS: Zones 3–8

BLOOM PERIOD: Midspring, late spring

SIZE: 8–36 in. high, 8–24 in. wide

H

Cool-season stunners, columbine thrives in the Northeast, and this fetching plant features some of the most intricate flowers in all horticulture. Columbine enjoys shady woodlands, and adapts to a range of soils. Most fade by summer and can be cut back, and some will seed around in the garden if they're especially content.

Native columbine *Aquilegia canadensis* grows large colonies in the wild and features red-hooded flowers of yellow. It grows 2–3 ft., while cultivar 'Little Lanterns' is the same at a third the size. Similar in size are varieties of European columbine (*A. vulgaris*) that bloom in a range of purply pinks and reds, including 'Black Barlow' in smoldering maroon. If it's blue you're after, try alpine columbine (*A. alpina*) or cultivars of fan columbine (*A. flabellata*). For sheer flower power, try plants in the Songbird series, like red 'Cardinal' and white 'Dove', with huge, 3 in. flowers that face upward.

Columbine (*Aquilegia* cultivar).

Camassia leichtlinii

Camassia

HARDINESS: Zones 5–9

BLOOM PERIOD: Midspring, late spring

SIZE: 3–4 ft. high, 1–2 ft. wide

D

Want to grow a rain garden? Camassia is the bulb for you. This blue-flowered plant blooms with cheery springtime spikes, and prefers soil that's damp to wet at that time of year, but dries out as summer sets in. Like many spring bulbs, its foliage declines and dies back post-bloom. Camassia fits right in along wetlands and ponds.

Camassia (*Camassia leichtlinii*).

Centaurea montana and cultivars

Mountain bluet

HARDINESS: Zones 3–8

BLOOM PERIOD: Late spring, early summer

SIZE: 6–12 in. high, 12–18 in. wide

D

Mountain bluet (*Centaurea montana*) blooms in spring, its flowers purple-centered eyes surrounded by petals of wispy blue, all above fuzzy, vaguely silver foliage. Bluet adores cooler climates and lean soils, and seeds around and spreads from the roots when conditions are right—deadhead to prevent seeding. Cultivar 'Amethyst in Snow' sports white petals instead of blue, and 'Gold Bullion' cuts a sharp contrast with gold foliage.

Mountain bluet (*Centaurea montana*).

Chionodoxa species and cultivars

Glory of the snow

HARDINESS: Zones 3–8

BLOOM PERIOD: Early spring

SIZE: 6–8 in. high, 4–6 in. wide

H

It may be called glory of the snow, but this bitsy bulb typically blooms a bit after winter's white blanket has melted, though it's completely unbothered by late-season snow. *Chionodoxa* blooms in blue, pink, purple, or white, and since its grassy foliage disappears by summer, it makes a fantastic bulb to scatter in lawn that isn't too dense. It also isn't bothered by rodents. Plant 3 in. deep in fall.

Glory of the snow (*Chionodoxa luciliae*).

Convallaria majalis and cultivars

Lily of the valley

HARDINESS: Zones 3–8

BLOOM PERIOD: Midspring, late spring

SIZE: 6–12 in. high, indefinite spread

H

Grow lily of the valley for its fresh, bold foliage and fragrant bells of pure white in spring to early summer, but be mindful of where you plant it, because this little groundcover lives up to that role, spreading to form a neat swath when conditions permit. Lily of the valley makes itself at home in woodland settings, but beware of dry shade if you'd like it to stick around—it will die back after blooming in droughty conditions. *Convallaria majalis* var. *rosea* blooms pink.

Lily of the valley (*Convallaria majalis*).

COOL-SEASON ANNUALS

While many an annual must wait for summer's heat, the wise gardener knows quick color is available early in the season, too, and much of it from plants that reseed for next year. Tulips, too, are often treated as annuals, though they're technically bulbs, as many showy varieties last one to two years, at best. Reseeders shown here are marked with an asterisk.

1. Snapdragon (*Antirrhinum* cultivar); 2. Dinosaur kale (*Brassica oleracea* 'Lacinato'); 3. Blue shrimp plant* (*Cerinthe major* 'Purpurescens'); 4. Sweet pea* (*Lathyrus odoratus* cultivar); 5. Love-in-a-mist* (*Nigella damascena* cultivar); 6. Breadseed poppy* (*Papaver somniferum* cultivar); 7. Nasturtium* (*Tropaeolum majus*); 8. Tulip (*Tulipa* cultivar); 9. Pansy (*Viola* cultivar).

Corydalis species and cultivars

Corydalis

HARDINESS: Zones 3/4/6–8

BLOOM PERIOD: Midspring, early summer, midsummer, late summer, fall

SIZE: 1–2 ft. high and wide

H

Fans of bleeding heart (*Dicentra* species) will love this dainty, early-blooming cousin with tiny groups of flute-shaped flowers. All bloom mid- to late spring and sporadically through fall, and grow easily in average to moist, well-drained soil in shade. Like its cousin, corydalis goes dormant in drier soils in the heat of summer. *Corydalis lutea* flowers yellow and spreads by seed, while cultivars of *C. solida* bloom white, pink, or purple. Both are hardy to Zone 3. Yellow-flowered *C. cheilanthifolia* (Zone 4) has the ferniest leaves, a foliar accent all season. Cultivars of Zone 6–hardy *C. flexuosa* feature flowers of blue.

'Blue Panda' corydalis (*Corydalis flexuosa* 'Blue Panda').

Fritillaria species and cultivars

Fritillary

HARDINESS: Zones 4/5–8

BLOOM PERIOD: Midspring, late spring, early summer

SIZE: 8 in.–4 ft. high, 8 in.–2 ft. wide

H

With a name as quirky as fritillary, a plant had better be beautiful. Fortunately for them (and gardeners), these bulbs are some of the most beautiful oddballs you could grow. The three species listed here have a few things in common: they prefer well-drained soil, and their crowns tend to collect water, causing rot, so it's best to plant them on their sides. All die back after blooming in spring.

Crown imperial (*Fritillaria imperialis*).

How about a flower with a crown of leaves? Crown imperial (*Fritillaria imperialis*, Zone 5) sends up tall stems that would appear to be pineapples on sticks—a 4-ft. whirl of nodding flowers in shades of orange, red, or yellow, all topped by a wild crown of green foliage. This king of flowering funk does best in sun in the Northeast, although it appreciates shade in the hottest part of the day. Crown imperial bulbs may be big, but they're breakable, so plant carefully in one spot and then leave them be. Also tall but more refined, Persian lily (*F. persica*, Zone 5) blooms with 3-ft. nodding bells of powdery purple. As its name suggests, this bulb hails from the Middle East, and as such, it prefers a hot, dry site. Persian lily grows best in full sun in cool summer regions here in the Northeast; give it afternoon shade in warmer Zone 7. Not to be outdone by its flashier cousins, checker lily's (*F. meleagris*) flowers come in checkered purple and coordinating white. The hardiest of the bunch, to Zone 4, it grows to around a foot, and prefers more shade.

Checker lily (*Fritillaria meleagris*)

Hyacinthoides hispanica and cultivars

Spanish bluebell

HARDINESS: Zones 3–8

BLOOM PERIOD: Midspring, late spring

SIZE: 12–18 in. high, 8–12 in. wide

H

Easy, underused, long-lived, and vaguely exotic, Spanish bluebells bring an easy grace to the pastel palette of the spring garden. This bulb's loose spikes of lavender flowers are streaked in sky blue, and cultivars also come in pink, white, and other shades of blue. Bluebell offsets to form stout clumps, resists rodents, and makes a pretty cut flower. Like most other spring bulbs, this Spanish stunner goes dormant when summer's heat sets in. Plant 4–5 in. deep in fall.

Spanish bluebell (*Hyacinthoides hispanica*).

Hyacinthus orientalis and cultivars

Dutch hyacinth

HARDINESS: Zones 4–8

BLOOM PERIOD: Midspring

SIZE: 8-12 in. high, 4-6 in. wide

D

Dutch hyacinth greets spring with cylindrical flowers and intoxicating fragrance, and cultivars of this popular bulb bloom in a cadre of cool purples and blues, white, pink, and pale yellow. Plant bulbs 4–6 in. deep in fall, in a sunny spot that gets spring rain but dries out in summer. Hyacinth is somewhat rodent-resistant, but benefits from being mixed with other, more vole-repellent plants that bloom later, like alliums. Deadhead after bloom; flower power tends to taper off after a few years, so they're a good fit for gardeners who like to change things up.

Dutch hyacinth (*Hyacinthus orientalis*).

Leucojum aestivum and cultivars

Summer snowflake

HARDINESS: Zones 4–8

BLOOM PERIOD: Early spring, midspring

SIZE: 12–18 in. high, 8–12 in. wide

H

Its common name may say summer, but this little snowflake definitely blooms in spring. This bulb's white flowers make for great drifts. Plant a few dozen, and they'll soon settle in and multiply for a snowy spring display you're more likely to appreciate than real snow. Summer snowflake goes dormant by midsummer; plant 3–4 in. deep in fall.

Summer snowflake (*Leucojum aestivum*).

Mertensia virginica

Virginia bluebell

HARDINESS: Zones 3–8

BLOOM PERIOD: Early spring, midspring

SIZE: 1–2 ft. high and wide

Don't let Virginia bluebell fool you—its flowers may start out a bit pink, but in the end, this belle is true blue. An easy native in cool, damp woodland conditions, Virginia bluebell makes a great choice in shady gardens with other perennials that may emerge later to take the spotlight by the time it goes dormant midsummer.

Virginia bluebell (*Mertensia virginica*).

Muscari armeniacum and cultivars

Grape hyacinth

HARDINESS: Zones 4–8

BLOOM PERIOD: Early spring, midspring

SIZE: 6–8 in. high, 4–6 in. wide

A spring mainstay and one of the easiest bulbs to grow, grape hyacinth brings cool hues to the typically vivid spring palette, its flowers like tiny upturned bunches of purple fruit. Cultivar 'Valerie Finnis' shines in sky blue, while indigo 'Blue Spike', makes ruffly double flowers that last longer. Grape hyacinth goes dormant in summer, but its grassy (sometimes messy) foliage reappears in fall and sticks around again until spring. Plant it 3–4 in. deep, and with partners, or even in lawn, to allow its leaves to blend easily.

Grape hyacinth (*Muscari armeniacum*).

Narcissus species and cultivars

Daffodil and narcissus

HARDINESS: **Zones 4–8**

BLOOM PERIOD: **Early spring, Midspring, late spring**

SIZE: **6–24 in. high, 6–12 in. wide**

H ☀ ◐ 🌡 🦌

Forsythia may rule when it comes to yellow in spring shrubs, but daffodil rules overall in spring yellows. This most familiar of bulbs grows easily in all kinds of situations, and comes in a range of sunny hues and sizes—yellow, as well as white, pink, and every combo in between. Larger plants go by the common name daffodil, while those in miniature are typically referred to as narcissus. All are legendary for repelling rodents, and can be planted in concert with other, tastier bulbs for this purpose. Countless cultivars exist, but culture for all is easy peasy and basically the same:

Start with full sun to part sun and well-drained soil. Plant in fall, three times deeper than the bulb's height, and leave the space of a couple bulbs in between—don't overcrowd. Once daffs are done blooming, let their foliage grow until it yellows. After that it can be cut back—usually around July 4—but cutting back sooner means the leaves can't recharge the bulbs' batteries, and they may not bloom next year.

If you find your daffs don't bloom, this could be why. Other common reasons: they're overcrowded (divide every 3 to 5 years); the soil they're planted in is too rich in nitrogen, which makes for more leaves instead of flowers; or their soil is nutrient-poor. For the most part, daffodils and narcissus are no-brainers, and a rite of spring for many a great garden.

Daffodil (*Narcissus* cultivar).

Primula species and cultivars

Primrose

HARDINESS: Zones 4–8

BLOOM PERIOD: Midspring, late spring, early summer

SIZE: 4–18 in. high, 6–12 in. wide

D

A true garden classic, primroses bring a rainbow of spring color to wet woodlands and pond edges. These plants vary a bit in looks, but all thrive in the cool climate of the Northeast, in damp soil and shade.

The tall members of the clan, drumstick primroses (*Primula denticulata*) push their pom-poms of flowers up on little green stalks in spring, and bloom in hues of lavender to white, some almost red. *P. japonica* (sometimes called Japanese primrose) makes a similar flower, more often red, and its leaves are bigger, like loose heads of lettuce.

Sometimes icons come in tiny packages, and English primrose (*Primula vulgaris*)—a plant grown in gardens as long as gardening has been a tradition—is surely a mini-icon. This little plant greets the season with a hummock of bright flowers, pale yellow in the species, and an array of other colors in cultivars. If it's a perennial plant you're after, be sure to shop for varieties with *P. vulgaris* in the botanical name, as polyanthus primroses (hybrids of *P. vulgaris* and *P. veris*) often sold as houseplants are referred to as English primroses, too.

Drumstick primrose (*Primula denticulata* cultivar).

English primrose (*Primula vulgaris* cultivar).

Pulmonaria species and cultivars

Lungwort

HARDINESS: Zones 4–9

BLOOM PERIOD: Late spring, early summer

SIZE: 6–12 in. high, 1–3 ft. wide

An easy plant for moist soil and shade, lungwort makes an enchanting alternative to the usual spring flowers, with tiny clumps of tubular trumpets in colors from red to pink and blue. In damp, shady sites, silvery, speckled leaves carry on even after it flowers, although lungwort goes dormant in dry soil.

Lungwort (*Pulmonaria* cultivar).

Scilla siberica

Siberian squill

HARDINESS: Zones 4–8

BLOOM PERIOD: Midspring

SIZE: 3–4 in. high and wide

A dose of Siberian squill's deep blue is just what the doctor ordered on those overcast spring days when winter won't quite let go. A common sight dotting lawns in the Northeast, this long-lived little bulb makes an ideal candidate to turn loose among groundcovers of all kinds, its foliage nondescript and dormant by summer. Better yet, squill repels rodent pests. Plant 2–3 in. deep in fall.

Siberian squill (*Scilla siberica*).

Trillium species

Trillium

HARDINESS: **Zones 3–8**

BLOOM PERIOD: **Midspring, late spring, early summer**

SIZE: **6–18 in. high, 6–12 in. wide**

H

Trillium is an untapped treasure for most gardeners, but those in the know are mad for this sophisticated spring ephemeral. A Northeast native, trillium adores shade and damp soil, and various species can be found growing in wet woodlands here and across North America. Leave trillium to grow once it's planted, and it spreads to form spectacular clumps. Species include white trillium (*Trillium grandiflorum*), whose ghostly flowers look like dogwood, and age from white to pink, and red trillium (*T. erectum*), which holds its maroon flowers high. Smaller yellow trillium (*T. luteum*) and red-flowering toadshade (*T. sessile*) make up for their size in spades with mottled, marbled leaves.

White trillium (*Trillium grandiflorum*).

'Flaming Purissima' Fosteriana tulip (*Tulipa fosteriana* 'Flaming Purissima').

Tulipa species and cultivars

Species tulip

HARDINESS: **Zones 3–8**

BLOOM PERIOD: **Early spring, midspring**

SIZE: **8–24 in. high, 6–24 in. wide**

H ☀ ◐ ≡ 🌡

Think tulips, and you're conjuring a Dutch landscape with fields of bright, nodding flowers and windmills, but did you know that those typical tulips only bloom once, maybe twice? After that, you'd best dig them up, because their unpretty foliage, sans flower, will return for many years. These tulips are best treated as annuals (see "Cool-Season Annuals," page 125). Fortunately, good news is here for we tulip fans who'd rather plant once, in the form of "species" tulips: cultivars of other, lesser known tulip species that return year after year, many very similar to our beloved annuals. All ask only sun and well-drained soil that dries out in summer—no watering! You'll find many others at your market. Tired of digging old tulips? Give species tulips a try.

Fosteriana tulip (*Tulipa fosteriana*) blooms midspring, its flowers open wide on sunny days, and cultivars of this taller tulip pass easily for annual cousins. Greigii tulip (*T. greigii*) mirrors those in miniature. Foliage of this tulip's squat cultivars features mottled spots and stripes, a treat after flowers fade. Tiny dynamo *T. bakeri* 'Lilac Wonder' blooms bicolor pink with yellow center, and *T. tarda* clear yellow.

EARLY TO MIDSUMMER

Blooming Abundance

Flowering plants take their long awaited turn at the microphone the first half of summer in the Northeast—they've been waiting, we've been waiting, and this is when they truly sing. The plants in this section step up at a time of year when we're stepping out, setting up shop for the growing season ahead and brimming with anticipation for it. It's no wonder they include some of the most beloved garden plants of all.

TREES, SHRUBS, AND VINES

Clematis species and cultivars

Clematis

HARDINESS: Zones 4–9

BLOOM PERIOD: Early summer, midsummer, late summer

SIZE: 3–10 ft. high and wide

D

A many and varied group of woody vines, clematis is the most beloved clan of climbers in the cool climate garden. While a few vines tolerate shade, most spend their lives clambering to the sun, and clematis is no exception: it prefers its feet in cool, average to moist, well-drained soil, and its face in the sun, so a

Fringed bleeding heart (*Dicentra*) and bluestar (*Amsonia*) bloom with northern maidenhair (*Adiantum*) and other ferns.

'Nelly Moser' clematis (*Clematis* 'Nelly Moser').

'Rooguchi' clematis (*Clematis* 'Rooguchi').

good mulch and a not-too-dry site are key. Clematis also prefer not to be moved, so try to plant them where they can stay long-term.

The traditional large-flowering clematis is a classic, classy vine, climbing primly up any neighboring structure it can wrap a tendril around, and promising a powerful floral show in early summer once it settles in. Vivacious cultivars may be single or double flowered, and come in every shade of these colors and many in between: pink ('Nelly Moser', 'Comtesse de Bouchaud'); blue ('Vyvyan Pennell'); purple ('Etoile Violette', classic 'Jackmanii'); along with white ('Miss Bateman'), red ('Madame Julia Correvon'); and even pale yellow ('Wada's Primrose').

On the other hand, if clematis played football, small-flowered vines of Integrifolia Group go long. Rather than a short period of bawdy blooms, Integrifolia clematis kicks off an extended season in early summer, with hundreds of small flowers, often all the way to frost. Cultivar 'Rooguchi' does it best, with wave after wave of blue-purple bells. At the end of the season, this clematis dies almost to the ground—cut it to within 1 ft. in late winter.

Hydrangea species and cultivars

Bigleaf hydrangea, smooth hydrangea, and mountain hydrangea

HARDINESS: Zones 3/5–9

BLOOM PERIOD: Midsummer, late summer

SIZE: 3–5 ft. high and wide

D

This most beloved genus of plants nationwide promises billowy clouds of bloom from summer through fall. The word hydrangea includes the Greek term *hydra*, which means water, a telltale sign that these plants aren't typically fans of drought. Most prefer shade in at least the heat of the day, and average to moist, well-drained soil.

Everyone's favorite hydrangea hands down, bigleaf *Hydrangea macrophylla* (Zone 5), is the mood ring of the plant kingdom, its flowers blue in acidic soil, pink in alkaline. A classic shrub for shade, bigleaf hydrangea will grow in sun in the cool summers of the Northeast, either in soil that's damp or seaside—it adores salt spray. Otherwise it wilts dramatically in midday sun, so stick with partial to full shade and average to moist, well-drained soil. *H. macrophylla* blooms on last year's wood, and flowering buds are often sacrificed to late frost. In our region, it's best to go with cultivars that bloom on new and old growth, like 'All Summer Beauty' and 'Penny Mac', as they bloom regardless. Mini varieties in the Everlasting series, like 'Revolution', top out at 3 ft., and flowers fade from solid blue or pink to a potpourri.

Bigleaf hydrangea (*Hydrangea macrophylla*).

'Invincibelle Spirit' smooth hydrangea (*Hydrangea arborescens* 'Invincibelle Spirit'). BELOW Mountain hydrangea (*Hydrangea serrata* cultivar).

Wishing for big, bold hydrangea, but stumped by winter cold and dry soil? You're in luck: cultivars of smooth hydrangea (*Hydrangea arborescens*) bloom with billowy flowers like its bigleaf cousin, weather short periods of drought with no problem, and they're cold-hardy to Zone 3. White giant 'Annabelle' makes an old-fashioned garden addition; 'Incrediball' also blooms white, but bigger. Newcomer 'Invincibelle Spirit' wows in pink, no matter soil pH. Smooth hydrangea takes full sun in moist soil—otherwise give it shade in the heat of the day. While less hardy, mountain hydrangea (*H. serrata*, Zone 5) comes in fabulous underused cultivars, like 'Bluebird', blooms in spite of chill, and thrives even in dry shade. This hydrangea sports hundreds of dainty lacecaps—big, sterile florets surrounding a constellation of fuzzy fertile flowers.

Kalmia latifolia and cultivars

Mountain laurel

HARDINESS: Zones 4–8

BLOOM PERIOD: Early summer

SIZE: 2–15 ft. high and wide

You're invited to mountain laurel's big top spectacular, a show that promises thousands of dazzlingly odd flowers in myriad hot hues, each shaped like an extraordinary circus tent in miniature. With age, this shrub also features furrowed, brown sugar bark. 'Sarah' sports red buds that open in pink, while dwarf 'Minuet' is white with a ring of claret around its center. 'Little Elf' blooms pure white, while 'Keepsake' is grape soda. A rhododendron relative, mountain laurel thrives in average to moist, acidic soil and part shade, but can stand up to a measure of drought once established.

Mountain laurel (*Kalmia latifolia* cultivar)

Lonicera species and cultivars

Honeysuckle

HARDINESS: **Zones 4/5–9**

BLOOM PERIOD: **Early summer, midsummer, late summer**

SIZE: **8–20 ft. high, 3–6 ft. wide**

D

Classic among climbers, honeysuckle blooms in summer with bright flowers, often fragrant, and comes in a grab bag of colors. This lively vine festoons anything in its path with woody stems, be it structure or shrub, so be sure to plant it someplace it can clamber with abandon. A fine vine for full sun, honeysuckle also grows well in part shade, but blooms best with light at least half the day.

Cultivars of Zone 4–hardy native trumpet honeysuckle (*Lonicera sempervirens*) bloom in a sunset array of red, orange, and yellow, much to the delight of hummingbirds for miles around. 'Major Wheeler' makes a powerful floral show, dripping with red flowers in summer, and sporadically until frost. For flower and fragrance, try varieties of European woodbine honeysuckle (Zone 5). One is old-fashioned *L. periclymenum* 'Serotina', with sweet-scented red and white bicolor blooms. *L.* ×*heckrottii* 'Gold Flame', features pink and yellow flowers.

Honeysuckle (*Lonicera* ×*heckrottii*).

Philadelphus species and cultivars

Mock orange

HARDINESS: **Zones 3–9**

BLOOM PERIOD: **Late spring, early summer**

SIZE: **6–8 ft. high and wide**

D ☀ ◐ ◑ ≡ 🌡 🦌

Tough as nails with a tender exterior, blooming mock orange makes a spectacular summer show coupled with clean green foliage and gray, exfoliating bark. Varied cultivars of this drought-resistant doily make it a good fit for gardens of all kinds. 'Innocence' and 'Belle Etoile' are fragrant, old-fashioned favorites, while double-flowered 'Miniature Snowflake' tops out at 3 ft. All-season 'Aureus' dazzles with lime foliage on top of flowers, while 'Variegatus' promises leaves boldly outlined in white.

Mock orange (*Philadelphus* species).

Rosa species and cultivars

Rose

HARDINESS: **Zones 3/5–10**

BLOOM PERIOD: **Early summer, midsummer, late summer, fall**

SIZE: **3–12 ft. high, 3–6 ft. wide**

D ☀ ◐ ≡

Rose claims the dubious distinction as one of the most popular and most finicky garden plants of all. Roses are undeniably glorious in bloom, which they do in early summer, but their list of demands and potential pests is too long for many a busy gardener. Fortunately, a world of low-maintenance roses has flooded the market, and given sun and average, rich soil, they make easy additions to any design. Many of these roses prove drought-resistant as well.

The popular Knock Out series comes in pink and red, as well as yellow, the best choice for fragrance. For a more old-fashioned look, choose a tough-but-tart polyantha rose like 'The Fairy', a small rose with bouquets of ruffly flowers that's almost everblooming. It's impossible not to love bulletproof cultivars

'The Knock Out' rose (*Rosa* 'The Knock Out').

of beach rose (*Rosa rugosa*) for cold climates and coastal gardens. Zone 3–hardy 'Hansa', a favorite, flowers in magenta. But what about a rose for foliage? *R. glauca* proves to be just that, with blue leaves tinged in red.

Climbing roses also tend to be more pest- and disease-resistant than their earthbound counterparts. Unlike vines that cling or twine, roses that climb do so with sprawling, thorny canes, so be ready to fasten them to a support as they grow. When pruning, leave at least a few feet of the plant's main canes—those that sprout near its base—and prune back lateral shoots that grow horizontally outward from these. Pruning can be done in early spring, before your rose leafs out, or after a flush of flower. Cultivars to try include 'Ballerina', 'New Dawn', 'Reve d'Or', and 'Sally Holmes'.

Beach rose (*Rosa rugosa*).

'The Fairy' polyantha rose (*Rosa* 'The Fairy').

Stewartia pseudocamellia

Stewartia

HARDINESS: Zones 5–9

BLOOM PERIOD: Early summer, midsummer

SIZE: 12–40 ft. high, 8–25 ft. wide

D

Imagine a camellia hardy enough to grow in your yard. Now imagine it grew to tree size, had beautiful bark, and fall leaves of red. Such a plant exists, and its name is stewartia. This small tree shines year-round but takes center stage in summer, when its "fried egg" flowers appear—pure white with buttery centers. Stewartia thrives in average to moist, well-drained soil, and asks for only a bit of shade in the hottest part of the day.

Stewartia (*Stewartia pseudocamellia*).

Styrax japonicus

Snowbell

HARDINESS: Zones 5–9

BLOOM PERIOD: Late spring, early summer

SIZE: 20–30 ft. high and wide

D

An Asian cousin of Carolina silverbell (*Halesia carolina*), snowbell flowers later, its branches crowded with blooms, like millions of tiny crocuses strung up on a summer tree. Most flower white, but cultivar 'Pink Chimes' blooms pink. Snowbell makes an easy small tree for average garden conditions.

'Pink Chimes' snowbell (*Styrax japonicus* 'Pink Chimes').

PERENNIALS, BULBS, AND ANNUALS

Acanthus spinosus

Acanthus

HARDINESS: Zones 5–10

BLOOM PERIOD: Early summer, midsummer

SIZE: 3–4 ft. high, 2–4 ft. wide

H

A treat in leaf as much as flower, acanthus makes a giant rosette of spiny, tropical-looking foliage, and blooms with ladders of purple or white in early summer. A Mediterranean plant, acanthus grows best in a garden spot where the soil warms early and stays that way, even though it tolerates a measure of shade.

Acanthus (*Acanthus spinosus*).

Achillea species and cultivars

Yarrow

HARDINESS: Zones 3–8

BLOOM PERIOD: Early summer, midsummer, late summer

SIZE: 2–4 ft. high and wide

H

A ferny, fine-textured plant for full sun, yarrow's bright bunches of bloom pepper gardens in early summer. Textural and traditional, its flowers come in an array of warm shades, from bright red and pastel yellow to linen white, and foliage varies from green to silver. Yarrow thrives in seaside gardens as well.

Yarrow (*Achillea* cultivar).

Allium species and cultivars

Allium

HARDINESS: **Zones 3/4/5–9**

BLOOM PERIOD: **Late spring, early summer**

SIZE: **8 in.–3 ft. high, 6–18 in. wide**

H

Odds are you've got an onion or two kicking around your kitchen for the sake of flavor—what about adding an onion or two to your garden for color and texture? Onions belong to the genus *Allium*, which includes many ornamental varieties known simply by that name. All are easy-to-grow bulbs that bloom in summer with spherical flowers and die back a bit afterward.

In the first half of summer, giant cultivars with names like 'Globemaster' (Zone 5) and 'Gladiator' (Zone 4) dot the landscape like purple disco balls on sticks. For a looser, more constellation-like globe, go with wild and woolly *Allium schubertii* (Zone 5), a treat into fall, long after flowers have dried. Drumstick allium (*A. sphaerocephalon*, Zone 4), a small, clumping garden classic, blooms in a multitude of maroon lollipops. *A. moly* (Zone 3) blooms yellow, with glossy green foliage that stays prettier longer, and even takes part shade.

Globe allium (*Allium* cultivar).

Allium schubertii.

Amsonia tabernaemontana and cultivars

Bluestar

HARDINESS: Zones 3–9

BLOOM PERIOD: Late spring, early summer

SIZE: 1–3 ft. high and wide

This type of bluestar proves to be the best flowering plant of its genus, and even takes shade, but makes a neater, more rounded silhouette in sun. A Northeast native, it also puts up with drought once it gets settled in. The species tops out at 3 ft., while compact cultivar 'Blue Ice' blooms in deeper, more lavender blue, and matures to 18 in. Foliage makes a terrific foil for other flowering plants through the growing season, and turns a delicious gold in fall.

Bluestar (*Amsonia tabernaemontana*).

Arisaema species and cultivars

Jack-in-the-pulpit

HARDINESS: Zones 4–9

SIZE: 12–24 in. high, 12–18 in. wide

Jack-in-the-pulpit (*Arisaema triphyllum*) is the odd Zone 4–hardy native that manages to cut a tropical silhouette, its flowers like tiny cobras peeking out from beneath one or two bold leaves. Gorgeous non-native cousins *A. sikkokianum* (Zone 5) and *A. ringens* (Zone 6) make garden-worthy additions too. All adore shade and damp to wet soil rich in organic matter, produce pretty red fruit after flowering, and then go dormant midsummer.

Jack-in-the-pulpit (*Arisaema triphyllum*).

Arum italicum

Italian arum

HARDINESS: Zones 5–9

BLOOM PERIOD: Late spring, early summer

SIZE: 12–18 in. high and wide

A beautiful trickster, Italian arum shines as a foliage plant, with exotically marbled leaves from spring into early summer, after its spring bloom of white-hooded flowers. After that, its leaves die back in summer's heat, but odd bouquets of orange fruit remain, a bizarre bookmark for a new foliar flush in fall. Italian arum thrives in average to moist soil and shade, and will make its way around the garden in ideal conditions, so give it room to colonize.

Italian arum (*Arum italicum*).

Aruncus species and cultivars

Goatsbeard

HARDINESS: Zones 4–8

BLOOM PERIOD: Late spring, early summer

SIZE: 1–6 ft. high, 1–4 ft. wide

Like a giant astilbe on steroids, native goatsbeard (*Aruncus dioicus*) shoots up to 6 ft. tall and blooms with ethereal, ostrich-ivory plumes in summer. It reaches full size and potential in damp soil, but adapts just fine to dry, and meshes well with design styles from cottage to exotic. Its non-native dwarf cousin, *A. aethusifolius*, does the same on a micro scale, growing scarcely over 1 ft. It eschews dry soil, and works perfectly as edging.

Goatsbeard (*Aruncus dioicus*).

Asclepias species

Milkweed

HARDINESS: Zones 3–10

BLOOM PERIOD: Early summer, midsummer

SIZE: 1–4 ft. high, 1–3 ft. wide

H

A low-water plant and an essential in any wildlife garden, milkweed may be among the most "green" perennials you could grow. Known first and foremost as dinner for monarch butterfly caterpillars, milkweed also blooms with exotic, weird flowers. It's best in average to dry soil and full sun.

The plant most known by the common name "milkweed" in the Northeast, *Asclepias syriaca* can get busy in the garden, but it's well worth it for its phenomenal pink flowers and pseudo-tropical silvery foliage. Plant someplace it can colonize, or snip seedheads and suckers to prevent its spread. A smaller, more proper member of the milkweed clan known as butterfly weed, *A. tuberosa* blooms orange in summer, starting early, but continuing intermittently all the way to fall. Be sure to give it dry soil and sun, as this little weed dislikes damp.

Butterfly weed (*Asclepias tuberosa*).

Astrantia major and cultivars

Masterwort

HARDINESS: Zones 4–7

BLOOM PERIOD: Late spring, early summer, midsummer

SIZE: 2–3 ft. high, 1–2 ft. wide

H

Cultivars of masterwort promise outrageous pincushions of bloom held high above maple-shaped leaves in early summer, and in shades of dark mauve, pink, and white. This plant prefers the cool twilight zone at the edge of damp woodland, so be sure to give it protection from harsh afternoon sun.

Masterwort (*Astrantia major* cultivar).

Baptisia species and cultivars

Baptisia

HARDINESS: Zones 3–9

BLOOM PERIOD: Late spring, early summer

SIZE: 3–4 ft. high and wide

H

In the span of one spring, baptisia grows up from nothing into a big, boxwood-like dome of blue-green, a simple solution for those who'd like the tidiness of shrubs but garden in lean soil. This drought-resistant perennial does it with a deep taproot and the ability to fix nitrogen from poor soil, like other members of the pea family, to which it belongs.

'Purple Smoke' baptisia (*Baptisia* 'Purple Smoke').

Even better, baptisia flowers in early summer with candles of elegant bloom, and cultivars today come in a rainbow of hues. Classic native *Baptisia australis* is decked out in blue, *B. alba* in white. Cultivar 'Cherries Jubilee' blooms red, 'Purple Smoke' is lavender with purple legs, and 'Twilite Prairieblues' flowers purple-black with foliage in an eye-catching blue. 'Carolina Moonlight' shimmers in pale yellow; 'Screaming Yellow' does the opposite.

Since baptisia grows deep roots, it won't look its best in nursery pots, but plant one in fall and you'll marvel at what a presence it is the next season. This plant is a cinch in sun and average to dry, well-drained soil.

Callirhoe involucrata

Wine cups

HARDINESS: Zones 4–9

BLOOM PERIOD: Late spring, early summer

SIZE: 6–12 in. high, 12–36 in. wide

This small poppy's strategy for growth is long and low, spreading out from its center to weave politely among neighbors. It could easily go unnoticed until it blooms—that's when its deep claret cups of flower demand attention. An excellent drought-resistant plant for full sun, it needs well-drained soil, and as a taprooted plant, it should be sited with care for the long-term.

Wine cups (*Callirhoe involucrata*).

Campanula species and cultivars

Bellflower

HARDINESS: Zones 3/5–8

BLOOM PERIOD: Late spring, early summer, midsummer

SIZE: 6 in.–4 ft. high, 1–3 ft. wide

H

In the bellflower family tree, you'll find aunts and uncles that are unmistakably related, but come in all shapes and sizes. The giveaway is those bell-shaped flowers, quite often in blue or white. Most make easy additions to the extended family of your garden, in full sun to part shade and average soil.

Two stand out in the small world of groundcover bellflowers. *Campanula carpatica* blooms with small, upturned bells, while *C. poscharskyana* flowers in six-petaled stars. Both hug the earth and spread well to cover it, like all bellflowers. *C. carpatica* 'Blue Clips' and 'White Clips' bloom accordingly, while 'Blue Waterfall' and 'Blue Gown' are popular cultivar choices in its cousin.

In mid-sized bellflowers, a few cultivars around 1 ft. stand out for the vividness of their blues. 'Viking' is a sterile hybrid of *Campanula punctata*, a beloved plant bemoaned for excessive spreading. This blue-lavender wonder spreads at a most modest clip. Taller 'Freya', at 16 in., comes from *C. glomerata*.

A few 4-ft. bellflowers might be called bell towers. Cultivars of *Campanula persicifolia* line tall stems with distinctly rounded, outward-facing bells. Popular choices include 'Telham Beauty' in blue and 'Chettle Charm' in white, and keep an eye out, because these bellflowers spread if conditions are favorable. A tall, sterile hybrid of two other species, 'Kent Belle' (Zone 5) features dangling bells of deep blue-purple, and won't seed out. All ask for shade from hot afternoon sun.

Bellflower (*Campanula persicifolia* cultivar).

'Kent Belle' bellflower (*Campanula* 'Kent Belle').

Coreopsis species and cultivars

Coreopsis

HARDINESS: Zones 3/4/5–9

BLOOM PERIOD: Early summer, midsummer, late summer

SIZE: 1–2 ft. high and wide

A treat for summer, coreopsis's hot-hued daisies mean hot weather is here to stay. Though it may come in different forms with different names, varieties of this plant want four things above all: sun, sun, sun, and average, well-drained soil. All may also be sheared back after bloom to keep them tidy.

For a fine-textured confection, look no further than cultivars of Zone 3–hardy threadleaf coreopsis (*Coreopsis verticillata*), a frothy mass of sweet yellow flowers above needled leaves. It excels even in dry soils. 'Moonbeam' blooms in pale yellow, while 'Zagreb' is gold. Pink-flowered *C. rosea* and its rosy cultivars may be visually similar, but dislike drought. If you want flashier flowers, try the bold, Zone 5–hardy daisies of the Big Bang series, like 'Full Moon' and 'Galaxy', or Zone 4–hardy *C. grandiflora* types like 'Early Sunrise'.

'Moonbeam' threadleaf coreopsis (*Coreopsis verticillata* 'Moonbeam').

Dianthus hybrids and cultivars

Pink

HARDINESS: Zones 3–8

BLOOM PERIOD: Late spring, early summer, midsummer

SIZE: 6–18 in. high, 8–18 in. wide

As its common name suggests, pink comes in a hot patchwork of that color, plus red and white. All bloom in a bawdy blanket above fetching blue-gray foliage and the smell of cloves. Pink prefers sun and lean, well-drained soil, and works well as a groundcover. 'Firewitch' is a classic short type in clear pink; 'Wicked Witch' is the same in red, 'Frosty Fire' redder still. In taller varieties, 'First Love' makes a pretty display with a sea of flowers that fade white to pink; 'Coconut Surprise' blooms red-eyed white, 'Peppermint Star' bicolor cherry and bubblegum.

Pink (*Dianthus* cultivar).

Dicentra species and cultivars

Bleeding heart

HARDINESS: **Zones 3–9**

BLOOM PERIOD: **Late spring, early summer, midsummer**

SIZE: **1–3 ft. high and wide**

H

What would a woodland garden be without bleeding heart? These shady characters bloom early summer with spectacular 3-D hearts, like pendant jewelry, each with a fully formed "drop" dripping from its center. Bleeding heart comes in big and small, but one thing's certain: sun typically sends it packing the rest of the growing season. Give it shade, and it's more likely to stick around.

Traditional favorite bleeding heart (*Dicentra spectabilis*) makes a bold showing by early summer, its 3-ft.-long arms and dripping wands of bloom reaching up from the forest floor. It comes in deep pink and white, and dies back by midsummer, unless it's provided with shade and cool, moist woodland conditions. Cultivar 'Gold Heart' electrifies dark corners with chartreuse foliage to go with those pink flowers, and it's also more likely to stick around through summer's heat. You may find it sold as *Lamprocapnos spectabilis*.

Fringed bleeding heart (*Dicentra eximia*) continues to be more fringy than its big cousin in terms of acceptance, but it's too bad—cultivars of this native dynamo are tougher, take more sun, and keep on ticking the entire growing season in shade and average to moist soil. More than that, its feathery, fine-textured foliage is pretty even when it isn't blooming. The species blooms in pink, white, or lavender. In hybrid cultivars, 'King of Hearts' flowers in vivid dark pink above blue leaves, and 'Burning Hearts' in a deeper red, with especially filigreed foliage.

Bleeding heart (*Dicentra spectabilis*).

Fringed bleeding heart (*Dicentra eximia* cultivar).

Dictamnus albus

Gas plant

HARDINESS: Zones 3–9

BLOOM PERIOD: Early summer

SIZE: 2–3 ft. high, 1–2 ft. wide

A shrub-sized perennial with scores of pink spikes in early summer, gas plant gets its name from oils it produces that are said to be flammable. (Don't try this at home.) Its foliage and flowers have a fresh, lemony scent, but look, don't touch: those same oils can irritate skin. Gas plant is another large perennial that grows a deep taproot, so it may not be the prettiest in a nursery pot. Plant as an investment in a sunny spot it can settle into for the long-term, and you'll be rewarded with years of flowers and crisp foliage.

Gas plant (*Dictamnus albus*).

Digitalis species and cultivars

Foxglove

HARDINESS: Zones 4–8

BLOOM PERIOD: Late spring, early summer

SIZE: 2–7 ft. high, 1–4 ft. wide

Foxglove spends its first year as a prim rosette of leaves, but the following year it sends up those famed skyrockets of flower in rosy pink, yellow and white, beloved and best known in cottage gardens. Foxglove is biennial, so the year after that, it may not return. Situate it in sun and soil of medium moisture (not too wet or dry), so it sets seed, and the cycle can begin again. All parts of foxglove are poisonous.

Foxglove (*Digitalis* cultivar).

Eryngium species and cultivars

Sea holly

HARDINESS: Zones 4/6–8

BLOOM PERIOD: Early summer, midsummer

SIZE: 1–3 ft. high and wide

Sea holly begins to bloom in summer, with iridescent, utterly unique flowers that carry the same substance as foliage, each one a fuzzy cone surrounded by shiny, spiky bracts. Each cultivar starts out white and matures to a slightly different shade of blue. 'Big Blue' (Zone 4) is a favorite today, a 3-ft. star for the middle of borders, while *Eryngium planum* 'Blue Hobbit' grows only 1 ft. 'Sapphire Blue' (Zone 5) comes in midway, at close to 30 in., as does *E. planum* 'Jade Frost', a foliar star with white-edged leaves. All sea hollies ask only sun and dry, well-drained soil.

Sea holly (*Eryngium* 'Sapphire Blue').

Geranium species and cultivars

Geranium

HARDINESS: Zones 3/4/5–8

BLOOM PERIOD: Late spring, early summer, midsummer

SIZE: 6–24 in. high, 6–18 in. wide

Not to be confused with popular annual geraniums, whose botanical name is *Pelargonium*, these little perennials have a devoted following all their own. Easy to grow in average garden conditions in sun to part shade, they carpet garden beds respectably, keeping out weeds while at the same time playing nice with other garden plants. Geraniums do best with a bit of shade in the hottest part of the day.

'Bevan's Variety' bigroot geranium (*Geranium macrorrhizum* 'Bevan's Variety').

The biggest, sturdiest geranium of all, bigroot geranium (*Geranium macrorrhizum*, Zone 4) shines even in dry shade. This geranium's substantial leaves make a perfect tableau for flashier plants above, and when it blooms, it has its moment of flash too. 'Ingwersen's Variety' flowers in pink that fades to white, while 'Bevan's Variety' blooms in bright rose. For a new flush of foliage after flower, shear bigroot to the ground after bloom. It may be unpretty for a brief period, but not for long.

Many small geranium cultivars prove to be showstoppers in the garden. Free-blooming 'Rozanne' (Zone 5) is most popular, a sun worshiper in lavender. Tiny varieties of *Geranium* ×*cantabrigiense* like 'Biokovo' (Zone 5) make impeccable mats of foliage, this one accented by pinky-white flowers. Zone 3–hardy cultivars of *G. sanguineum* bloom in clear pink. For foliage lovers, *G. phaeum* 'Samobor' (Zone 4) features purple-striped leaves, a treat with deep purple flowers.

'Rozanne' geranium (*Geranium* 'Rozanne').

Iris species and cultivars

Iris

HARDINESS: **Zones 3–10**

BLOOM PERIOD: **Late spring, early summer**

SIZE: **2–4 ft. high, 1–3 ft. wide**

The iris family is a many and varied group with two physical features that make them distinct: sword-like leaves, often a subtly bold vertical accent in the garden even when they're not in bloom; and more importantly, those distinct fleur de lis–shaped flowers, usually a group of big petals that point skyward encircled by a group that tumble gracefully down.

Bearded iris (*Iris* cultivar).

Most renowned are bearded irises (Zone 3), for their big petticoats of summer bloom in a spectrum of colors so huge you can take your pick. This iris adores sun and well-drained soil, and becomes drought-resistant with age. It grows from a creeping rhizome that's best not buried too deeply. Most bearded cultivars are hybrids whose botanical name will only be *Iris* and their cultivar name, so for once they're best identified at the nursery by the word "bearded" in their common name. Two exceptions are purple bearded irises grown as much for their variegated leaves: *Iris pallida* 'Variegata' (silvery white-striped) and *I. pallida* 'Aureovariegata' (striped in gold), both hardy to Zone 4. Bearded iris is best divided every few years to keep clumps from getting crowded.

Besides the bearded branch of the iris family, cultivars of Siberian iris (*Iris sibirica*, Zone 3) make equally garden-worthy additions—some might say better. This iris takes a wider range of cultural conditions including light shade and damp soil, its foliar swords stand taller and make a fabulous vertical accent, and its flowers recall a lively flock of colorful birds.

Siberian iris (*Iris sibirica* cultivar).

Lamium species and cultivars

Dead nettle

HARDINESS: Zones 3–8

BLOOM PERIOD: Late spring, early summer

SIZE: 6–10 in. high, 6–36 in. wide

H

Dead nettle makes a star turn as bulletproof, colorful carpet for shade, especially in spring and summer, when its white-variegated foliage is offset by flowers in jewel tones. It thrives in any shady situation besides extra-wet soil, and cultivars of *Lamium maculatum* are most common. 'White Nancy' and 'Red Nancy' are two classics with flowers to match and silver-centered leaves. A newer form, 'Ghost', ups the ante with all-white foliage along with pink flowers. These types are spreaders; best to let them colonize. If it's a polite, non-spreading clump you're after, go with *L. galeobdolon* 'Herman's Pride', a white-speckled vision with flowers of yellow. (Avoid the species; it can be weedy.)

'Herman's Pride' dead nettle (*Lamium galeobdolon* 'Herman's Pride').

Ligularia species and cultivars

Ligularia

HARDINESS: Zones 4–8

BLOOM PERIOD: Early summer, midsummer

SIZE: 2–5 ft. high, 2–4 ft. wide

H

The wild child of the wet garden, ligularia loves nothing better than damp soil and shade. It returns the favor with voluptuously fleshy leaves and loud yellow daisies, a statement you know your garden is asking for. Even better, *Ligularia dentata* 'Britt Marie Crawford' screams for attention with complementary purple-almost-black foliage. If you prefer a bigger plant with more flower power, try 'The Rocket' which has 5-ft. yellow spikes of bloom.

'Britt Marie Crawford' ligularia (*Ligularia dentata* 'Britt Marie Crawford').

Nepeta ×*faassenii* 'Walker's Low'

Catmint

HARDINESS: Zones 4–8

BLOOM PERIOD: Early summer, midsummer

SIZE: 2–3 ft. high and wide

H

An easy weed-busting groundcover, 'Walker's Low' catmint makes a dense, silver, cola-scented mat, topped off in summer with up to a month of lavender bloom. With a light shearing after it's done, it repeats the show by fall. Drought-resistant catmint is a cinch in sun and well-drained soil; it divides best in spring.

'Walker's Low' catmint (*Nepeta* ×*faassenii* 'Walker's Low').

Paeonia species and cultivars

Peony, tree peony

HARDINESS: Zones 3/4–8

BLOOM PERIOD: Early summer

SIZE: 2–5 ft. high, 2–4 ft. wide

D H

A beloved old-fashioned favorite, herbaceous peony (*Paeonia lactiflora* cultivars) blooms in early summer with giant, bowl-shaped flowers, often fragrant and seemingly lit from within. This beauty has more cultivars than you can shake a stick at, but all have a few things in common. They prefer sun to light shade and fertile, well-drained soil, and won't grow or bloom well if planted too deeply. Peony's leaves may be prone to powdery mildew late in the season.

Peony (*Paeonia* cultivar).

If infected, carefully remove powdered foliage when it's dry to keep from spreading the disease, and dispose of it by burying; composting it someplace away from plants, buried deep within the heap; or wrapping it up with the trash or yard waste, if your town offers pickup. Peony is also prone to flopping in the rain, so grow it for cutting, or install wire peony cages for plants to grow up through.

If you're tired of floppy peonies, woody tree peony (*Paeonia suffruticosa* cultivars) makes a tougher garden addition, as a shrub that doesn't die to the ground in winter. Even better, recent crosses between the two cousins have produced exciting new hybrids, like yellow-flowered 'Bartzella'. Called Itoh peonies, these plants promise all the oomph of tree types, but die back like their herbaceous cousins.

Papaver orientale and cultivars

Oriental poppy

HARDINESS: **Zones 3–7**

BLOOM PERIOD: **Early summer**

SIZE: **18–30 in. high, 18–24 in. wide**

H

A horticultural confection, Oriental poppy's hot-colored crepe petals whisper with summer intentions, but this plant can be finicky. First, start with full sun, a solid remedy for flopping. Second, soil must be well drained, especially in winter, to prevent rot. Finally, plan for dormancy with neighbors that mature mid- to late summer, as poppies may decide to bid you *adieu* post-bloom—or their leaves may get ratty, best to be hidden.

Oriental poppy (*Papaver orientale* cultivar).

Penstemon species and cultivars

Beardtongue

HARDINESS: Zones 3–8

BLOOM PERIOD: Midsummer

SIZE: 1–3 ft. high, 1–2 ft. wide

A perennial cousin of annual snapdragon (*Antirrhinum* cultivars), beardtongue blooms much like its relative, but in summer, with vertical, tubular ladders of flower. This plant does well in average to dry soil and sun, and makes a stellar addition to dry gardens. Most popular is *Penstemon digitalis* 'Husker Red', a white-flowered cultivar grown as much for devilishly purple foliage that fades slowly to green. Similar 'Dark Towers' blooms pink and holds its foliage color longer. In gardens up to Zone 6, try cultivars of *P. heterophyllus*, like 'Blue Springs, that blooms in ocean shades of clear blue. Other varieties come in red, pink, and purple.

'Husker Red' beardtongue (*Penstemon digitalis* 'Husker Red').

Phlox stolonifera and cultivars, *P. subulata* and cultivars

Woodland phlox, creeping phlox

HARDINESS: Zones 4–8

BLOOM PERIOD: Late spring, early summer, midsummer

SIZE: 4–12 in. high, 12–24 in. wide

H ☀ ◐ ☁ 🌡 🦌 📍

You may be more familiar with the mossy variety, but two types of creepers make great garden plants for the phlox-inclined: *Phlox subulata*, the familiar, lower-growing kind, and *P. stolonifera*, a blousier native sometimes called woodland phlox. The former thrives in sun, and carpets itself in a sheet of bloom. The latter prefers shade, and blooms in loose drumsticks. Both come in color cultivars in blue, pink, and white, and make perfect groundcovers. Both also withstand moderate drought once established.

Woodland phlox (*Phlox stolonifera* cultivar).

Creeping phlox (*Phlox subulata* cultivar).

Salvia species and cultivars

Sage

HARDINESS: Zones 4/5–8

BLOOM PERIOD: Early summer, midsummer

SIZE: 1–2 ft. high and wide

H

Though you may know sage for the culinary cousins on its family tree, many a sage is grown for ornament too. All are easy plants in sun and average soil, but excel in drought, and all promise deer resistance, given their aromatic leaves. *Salvia* ×*sylvestris* 'May Night' and *S. nemorosa* 'Caradonna' are popular purple-spiked cultivars, while 'Eveline' shines in pink. *S. verticillata* 'Purple Rain' (Zone 5) is a relative newcomer, with flower spikes studded in purple spheres of bloom.

'Caradonna' sage (*Salvia nemorosa* 'Caradonna').

'Purple Rain' sage (*Salvia verticillata* 'Purple Rain').

Thalictrum rochebruneanum

Meadow rue

HARDINESS: Zones 4–7

BLOOM PERIOD: Midsummer, late summer

SIZE: 3–6 ft. high, 2–3 ft. wide

Gentle giant meadow rue blooms in a purple haze of tiny flowers, all held atop skyrocket stems, like a model of the Milky Way. A must for gardeners who love big perennials, when it blooms, meadow rue's vertical presence is unmatched. Meadow rue works well with morning sun, and won't stand for drought. Its strong stems shouldn't need staking, but site away from windy spots for good measure.

Meadow rue (*Thalictrum rochebruneanum*).

Thermopsis caroliniana, *T. chinensis* 'Sophia'

False lupine

HARDINESS: Zones 4/5–9

BLOOM PERIOD: Midsummer

SIZE: 1–5 ft. high, 2–3 ft. wide

Every garden needs good spikes, and false lupine delivers in spades. This pea family perennial thrives in full sun, and blooms in summer with cheerful canary spires. At 5 ft., Carolina lupine (*Thermopsis caroliniana*, Zone 4) is a tall treat, while shorter 'Sophia' Chinese lupine (*T. chinensis*, Zone 5) brings all the flower power in a foot and a half. False lupine is easy in average to dry soil.

Carolina lupine (*Thermopsis caroliniana*).

Veronica species, hybrids, and cultivars

Veronica

HARDINESS: Zones 3/4/6–9

BLOOM PERIOD: Late spring, early summer, midsummer

SIZE: 6 in.–2 ft. high, 1–2 ft. wide

H

Also called speedwell, veronica comes in a couple of distinct types, and blooms over a long period throughout the growing season. The earlier bloomer, *Veronica peduncularis* (Zone 6), is a groundcover, and blooms from end of spring into early summer. Cultivar 'Georgia Blue' is most common, and an all-star with tiny, round flowers of clear blue. The later flowerer is a taller perennial with signature spikes—two familiar varieties are *V. spicata* 'Red Fox' (Zone 3) and hybrid 'Sunny Border Blue' (Zone 4). All are a cinch for early summer color in sun and average soil, and may bloom sporadically through the rest of the growing season.

Veronica (*Veronica peduncularis* cultivar).

TROPICALS

Gardening in the Northeast and growing tropical plants aren't mutually exclusive! A number of tropicals are perfectly content to grow like mad in the warm, humid summers of our region and rest indoors in the off-season.

1. Flowering maple (*Abutilon* cultivar);
2. 'Zwartkop' aeonium (*Aeonium arboreum* 'Zwartkop'). CONTINUED ON PAGE 168

TROPICALS

3. Agave (*Agave americana*); 4. Begonia (*Begonia* cultivar); 5. Bromeliad; 6. Brugmansia (*Brugmansia* cultivar); 7. Canna (*Canna* cultivar); 8. 'Nagami kumquat' (*Fortunella margarita* 'Nagami'); 9. Elephant ear (*Colocasia* cultivar); 10. Dahlia (*Dahlia* cultivar); 11. 'Sparkling Burgundy' pineapple lily (*Eucomis comosa* 'Sparkling Burgundy'); 12. Red banana (*Ensete ventricosum* 'Maurelii').

WARM-SEASON ANNUALS

With late frosts a thing of the past, summer is the time annuals truly come into their own. Any plant lover will be hard pressed to resist the temptation of exotic color served up by these vivid plants. Those that reseed for next season are marked with an asterisk.

1. Amaranth (*Amaranthus* cultivar)*; 2. Spider flower (*Cleome hassleriana* cultivar)*; 3 Cosmos (*Cosmos* cultivar)*; 4. Fuchsia (*Fuchsia* cultivar); 5. 'Strawberry Fields' globe amaranth (*Gomphrena haageana* 'Strawberry Fields'); 6. Annual sunflower (*Helianthus annuus* cultivar)*; 7. Heliotrope (*Heliotropium* cultivar); 8. New Guinea impatiens (*Impatiens* cultivar); 9. Sweet potato vine (*Ipomoea batatas* cultivar). CONTINUED ON PAGE 170

WARM-SEASON ANNUALS

10. Hyacinth bean (*Lablab purpureus*)*; 11. Mexican feather grass (*Nassella tenuissima*)*; 12. Flowering tobacco (*Nicotiana* cultivar)*; 13. African daisy (*Osteospermum* cultivar); 14. Geranium (*Pelargonium* cultivar); 15. Petunia (*Petunia* cultivar); 16. Plectranthus (*Plectranthus* cultivar); 17. Ptilotus 'Joey'; 18. Castor bean (*Ricinus communis* cultivar).

WARM-SEASON ANNUALS

19. Fan flower (*Scaevola* cultivar); 20. Coleus (*Solenostemon scutellarioides* cultivar); 21. Marigold (*Tagetes* cultivar); 22. Jewels of Opar (*Talinum* 'Limon')*; 23. Black-eyed Susan vine (*Thunbergia alata* cultivars); 24. Drumstick verbena (*Verbena bonariensis*)*; 25. Zinnia (*Zinnia* cultivar).

LATE SUMMER TO FALL

Floral and Foliar Fireworks

Though the hot palette that dominates late summer and fall signifies the inevitable end of the growing season, its reds, oranges, and yellows also refuse to be anything but joyful. Whether you see them as last hurrah or distraction from the coming winter, theirs is undeniably the most dramatic flourish of the growing season, and it's the best kind of garden drama to get swept up in.

TREES, SHRUBS, AND VINES

Red maple (*Acer rubrum*). OPPOSITE Daylily (*Hemerocallis*) blooms with red-leaved switch grass (*Panicum* cultivar) and other late season stars.

Acer species

Maple

HARDINESS: Zones 3–9

BLOOM PERIOD: Fall

SIZE: 40–80 ft. high, 30–60 ft. wide

D

Maples make fall the spectacle it is in the Northeast, and two species in particular contribute to the autumn show. Not to be confused with the Japanese species, native red maple (*Acer rubrum*) is a bigger tree, and gets its name both from its foliage that sets fall aflame and tiny flowers in spring that appear as a reddish haze before those leaves emerge. Red maple thrives in sites ranging from wet and mucky to streetside, once established. It grows 40–70 ft. Sugar maple (*A. saccharum*) burns in shades of gold to light orange in fall, and it's best known as the source of maple syrup. The larger of the two, it grows to 80 ft., prefers average soil, and needs more space to spread out.

Buddleia davidii cultivars

Butterfly bush

HARDINESS: Zones 5–9

BLOOM PERIOD: Midsummer, late summer, fall

SIZE: 6–8 ft. high, 3–5 ft. wide

D

Butterfly bush is a one-stop shop for pretty flowers, pollinators, and fragrance midsummer to fall. Given sun and average to dry soil, this cheery plant promises funnels of sweet flowers, and varieties come in a multitude of colors. 'Black Knight' is a time-tested favorite. Tough love works best for butterfly bush—trim it 12–18 in. from the ground in late winter to keep it shapely. Plants may spread by seed in the mildest seaside regions of the Northeast, so be watchful for unwanted babies.

Butterfly bush (*Buddleia davidii* cultivar).

Callicarpa species and cultivars

Beautyberry

HARDINESS: Zones 5/6–10

SIZE: 3–6 ft. high and wide

D

If you've got a thing for shrubs with bling, beautyberry should be at the top of your wish list. Varieties of this vase-shaped shrub produce berries of pink, purple, or white, and that shape is best maintained by chopping it to within a foot of the ground in late winter. Birds will be drawn to its berry-studded branches, and they'll make the neighbors swoon in combination with gold fall foliage. Look for cultivars 'Early Amethyst' (Zone 5) and 'Profusion' (Zone 6), or big-leaved native *Callicarpa americana* (Zone 6).

Beautyberry (*Callicarpa cultivar*).

Campsis species and cultivars

Trumpet creeper

HARDINESS: Zones 4/6–9

BLOOM PERIOD: Midsummer, late summer

SIZE: 20–40 ft. high, 5–10 ft. wide

D

A pseudo-tropical treat if you've got space to spare or need quick cover, trumpet creeper is famous for its tubular orange flowers, beloved by hummingbirds, and its tendency to grow like wildfire once it's settled in. Native *Campsis radicans* (Zone 4) is a fast and loud climber, while *C. grandiflora* 'Morning Calm' (Zone 6) is a less-hardy cultivar of an Asian species said to be tamer.

Trumpet creeper (*Campsis radicans*).

Caryopteris ×*clandonensis* cultivars

Bluebeard

HARDINESS: Zones 5–9

BLOOM PERIOD: Late summer, fall

SIZE: 2–4 ft. high and wide

D

Late summer plants that make their star turn in cool colors are always a refreshing contrast. Not only do bluebeard's chilly blue flowers fit the bill, they make a perfect complement to its silvery, frosted foliage. Bluebeard is a woody shrub, but it's best chopped to the ground in late winter, and may die back anyway in the northerly reaches of its range. It also winters better with well-drained soil. Leaves are lemon-scented. 'Longwood Blue' and 'Dark Knight' are two popular cultivars.

'Longwood Blue' bluebeard (*Caryopteris* ×*clandonensis* 'Longwood Blue').

Clethra alnifolia and cultivars

Summersweet

HARDINESS: Zones 3/4–9

BLOOM PERIOD: Midsummer, late summer

SIZE: 3–8 ft. high, 4–6 ft. wide

D

Summersweet's heady, spicy bouquet signals the turning point of that season toward fall, and it's fitting, since this shrub promises gold fall leaves, too. Summersweet blooms white, prefers some shade, and average to moist soil—it's a native plant, usually found around wetlands. Cultivar 'Ruby Spice' (Zone 4) blooms pink, and gardeners with less space should check out dwarf 'Hummingbird' at 4 ft.

Summersweet (*Clethra alnifolia*).

Ginkgo biloba

Ginkgo

HARDINESS: Zones 3–8

SIZE: 50–80 ft. high, 30–40 ft. wide

D

A relic left over from the days of dinosaurs, ginkgo brings a taste of the Jurassic to any garden. Though its deciduousness and fan-shaped leaves may lead you to believe otherwise, this odd tree is actually a conifer, and its overall shape is a clue to that. Ginkgo sparkles in fall with fabulous gold leaves. Easy in sun and any soil, it makes an ideal street tree.

Ginkgo (*Ginkgo biloba*).

Heptacodium miconioides

Seven son flower

HARDINESS: Zones 4–9

BLOOM PERIOD: Late summer

SIZE: 15–20 ft. high, 8–10 ft. wide

D

If you ask around among those in the know, you're bound to find seven son flower in everyone's top ten list of underused shrubs. This plant has it all, but truly shines late summer to fall, with billows of fragrant white bloom that give way to flower-like seedheads in magenta. It's a "wow" plant through the growing season with clean, dark green leaves, and year-round with extravagantly peeling bark in shades of tan to linen white. Seven son flower thrives in sun to part shade and most any soil, and looks best with a bit of pruning, which you can do in late winter.

Seven son flower (*Heptacodium miconioides*).

Hibiscus syriacus cultivars

Rose of Sharon

HARDINESS: Zones 5–8

BLOOM PERIOD: Late summer, fall

SIZE: 8–12 ft. high, 4–6 ft. wide

D

You may know hibiscus as a perennial or a tropical, but how about a shrub? Rose of Sharon is a woody hibiscus that blooms with wild, tropical flowers in the sweltering heat of late summer, usually during a lull for the rest of the garden. Some cultivars of this plant can seed around to excess, but classic 'Diana' shines in snow white, with darker, tidier foliage to boot, and is said to be sterile. A newer, less-weedy addition is 'Blue Satin', a rare near-clear blue. Drought-resistant rose of Sharon is easy in sun and adapts to a range of soil types.

'Diana' rose of Sharon (*Hibiscus syriacus* 'Diana').

Hydrangea paniculata and cultivars, *H. quercifolia* and cultivars

Panicle hydrangea, oakleaf hydrangea

HARDINESS: Zones 3/5–9

BLOOM PERIOD: Late summer, fall

SIZE: 8–15 ft. high, 6–12 ft. wide

D

Though their more popular relatives may bloom toward the middle of summer, two species keep the hydrangea party going all the way to frost—and prove to be tougher and more versatile, culturally and visually. For this group, prune out spent flowerheads in late winter, before the plants leaf out.

The first is panicle hydrangea (*Hydrangea paniculata*, Zone 3), a ruffled cloudburst of a plant when it blooms with white billows in late summer. Its cousins might prefer some shade during the day, but this hydrangea is A-OK in full sun. A common cultivar, 'Grandiflora' (often called "peegee" hydrangea) does the same, but with flowers that age to pink. These two can be grown as large shrubs (10 ft. or more) or even small trees. Too big? Try smaller 'Limelight', a spectacular bloomer with flowers that turn from white to chartreuse to rosy pink, or 'Quickfire',

Panicle hydrangea (*Hydrangea paniculata* cultivar).

in white to reddish-pink. This pair will grow to 8 ft. if you let them, but can be kept smaller.

Oakleaf hydrangea (*Hydrangea quercifolia*, Zone 5) is the other late-season species to love, as well as being one of the few hydrangeas to grow for foliage. It blooms in late summer with cones of ruffled white that age to pink, much like peegee, but this shrub also promises bold, fingered foliage bigger than your hand. These leathery leaves turn red-purple in fall. Oakleaf hydrangea is deer-resistant and likes shade best. For an even longer season of color, try dwarf, gold-leaved 'Little Honey'.

Oakleaf hydrangea (*Hydrangea quercifolia*).

Itea virginica and cultivars

Itea

HARDINESS: Zones 5–9

BLOOM PERIOD: Midsummer

SIZE: 3–5 ft. high, 3–6 ft. wide

D

Tough itea labors in obscurity until its time to shine, and when it does that, it takes center stage. Its first turn is midsummer, with flowing white tresses of fragrant flower, but the real treat is fall, when its foliage turns vividly red. 'Henry's Garnet' is a compact cultivar topping out at 4 ft., while 'Morton', also called 'Scarlet Beauty', is hardy to Zone 4. Itea thrives in a range of conditions, including wet soil (best for sun), and moderately dry in part shade.

Itea (*Itea virginica*).

Lespedeza thunbergii cultivars

Bush clover

HARDINESS: Zones 5–9

BLOOM PERIOD: Late summer, fall

SIZE: 4–5 ft. high, 5–10 ft. wide

D

Bulletproof bush clover weights itself with sheets of flowers in late summer, an ideal drought-tolerant accent shrub for tough slopes and walls. This easy shrub thrives most anywhere in sun to part shade, thanks to its pea family origins, which allow it to fix nitrogen from the soil. Cultivars include cumulus-colored 'White Fountain', and 'Gibraltar' in magenta. For a tidier plant, treat it like a perennial, and chop it down in late winter.

Bush clover (*Lespedeza thunbergii* cultivar).

Nyssa sylvatica

Tupelo

HARDINESS: Zones 3–9

SIZE: 30–50 ft. high, 20–30 ft. wide

Native tupelo can be found in wetlands across the East, but this adaptable tree proves drought-resistant too, and a vision in fall, when its glossy leaves turn an array of hot colors. Tupelo grows a deep taproot, which means it may need extra help getting settled in, and careful siting for the long-term. Its hidden flowers in spring are nonetheless a favorite of bees.

Tupelo (*Nyssa sylvatica*).

Oxydendrum arboreum

Sourwood

HARDINESS: Zones 5–9

BLOOM PERIOD: Midsummer

SIZE: 20–50 ft. high, 10–20 ft. wide

Sourwood gets the summer party started as a lacy layer cake of white flowers, followed by seed capsules that go perfectly with fire engine fall leaves. In between, its big, glossy leaves feel a bit tropical, but this underused small tree is a Northeast native. Bees flock to flowers, and sourwood honey is highly sought after. Sourwood works best in full sun and acidic soil, average to moist but well drained.

Sourwood (*Oxydendrum arboreum*).

Parrotia persica

Ironwood

HARDINESS: Zones 4–8

SIZE: 20–40 ft. high, 20–30 ft. wide

D

A spectacular underdog in the world of small trees, ironwood shines year-round, but especially in fall, when its glossy leaves turn from deep green to shades of hot citrus. On top of that, in spring, ironwood promises tiny, red, witch hazel–like flowers (it's a relative), and ornately textured gray bark flecked with white and tan. If you're not already convinced, ironwood adapts to all kinds of soils in full sun to part shade. What are you waiting for? There's sure to be a spot for ironwood in your garden.

Ironwood (*Parrotia persica*).

Parthenocissus quinquefolia, *P. tricuspidata*

Virginia creeper, Boston ivy

HARDINESS: Zones 3/4–9

SIZE: 30–50 ft. high, 5–10 ft. wide

D

A familiar native vine often uncharitably labeled "weed," Virginia creeper's (*Parthenocissus quinquefolia*, Zone 3) charms are due for a second look. It's an easy vine for sun or shade, with blue berries in late summer that birds adore, and fall foliage in sunset shades of red. Don't be afraid to prune this vigorous vine fearlessly. If its tendency to spread makes you nervous, try its European relative, Boston ivy (*P. tricuspidata*, Zone 4), a familiar vertical carpet of green on buildings in that city and elsewhere, with fall color of a similarly scarlet hue.

Boston ivy (*Parthenocissus tricuspidata*).

PERENNIALS

Aconitum species and cultivars

Monkshood

HARDINESS: Zones 3–7

BLOOM PERIOD: Late summer, fall

SIZE: 2–4 ft. high, 1–2 ft. wide

For plants, late summer and fall bring a palette of fiery hues, first in flower, and then in leaf. That's what makes monkshood's contrasting blooms in blue shades from deep ocean to azure sky an even more welcome sight. A plant best in cool, damp woodland soil, and shaded from midday heat, gorgeous monkshood is also poisonous. Plant it with care away from where children and pets may be tempted, and tend with gloves. Monkshood may be the last plant in the garden to bloom. *Aconitum napellus* blooms earlier, while cultivars in the Arendsii Group are last.

Agastache species and cultivars

Anise hyssop

HARDINESS: Zones 5–9

BLOOM PERIOD: Midsummer, late summer, fall

SIZE: 2–3 ft. high, 1–2 ft. wide

Pollinators go nuts for anise hyssop's azure flowers, another fine contrast with the typically fiery floral palette of late summer. 'Blue Fortune' and 'Black Adder', two hybrid cultivars of native and Asian species, promise an exceptionally excellent show. If you'd prefer showy foliage, go for smaller *Agastache foeniculum* 'Golden Jubilee', a chartreuse-leaved variety with pink flowers great for brightening light shade. All anise hyssops enjoy sun, heat, and soil that drains well, thriving in neglected droughty spots once established. These are tamer members of the mint family, less prone to spreading, but will indeed seed around a bit if conditions are right. That said, their mint-scented leaves keep furry pests at bay.

'Black Adder' anise hyssop (*Agastache* 'Black Adder').
LEFT Monkshood (*Aconitum* cultivar).

Anemone hupehensis and cultivars, *A.* ×*hybrida* and cultivars

Anemone

HARDINESS: Zones 5–7

BLOOM PERIOD: Late summer, fall

SIZE: 3–4 ft. high, 2–3 ft. wide

Tall anemones inject the fall plant palette with a bracing flash of white and pastel pink. *Anemone ×hybrida* cultivars like white 'Honorine Jobert' and pink 'Queen Charlotte' keep the color going from August through October. *A. hupehensis* var. *japonica* 'Bressingham Glow' and its brethren bloom in dark pink. These graceful, underused gems grow easily in average to moist, well-drained soil and light shade. More sun is okay with consistent moisture, but good winter drainage is a must, and an insulating mulch their first winter is a good idea.

Anemone (*Anemone* cultivar).

Aster species and cultivars, *Symphyotrichum* species and cultivars

Aster

HARDINESS: Zones 3/4–8

BLOOM PERIOD: Fall

SIZE: 1–4 ft. high, 1–3 ft. wide

'Purple Dome' aster (*Symphyotrichum novae-angilae* 'Purple Dome').

In the market for a fall-blooming mum alternative? Look no further than aster, its close relative, and a breath of fresh air come fall. Asters come in a range of shapes and sizes, but most greet fall with a sea of small daisies in fresh blues, pinks, and purples that contrast exquisitely with the hot-colored fall foliage of trees and shrubs. All were formerly included in the genus *Aster*, but today that typically refers only to Old World species, while most from the Americas are called *Symphyotrichum*. Still, we usually just call them asters, so I've gathered them together here.

New England aster (*Symphyotrichum novae-angliae*, Zone 3) is one of the natives, and cultivars of this plant like 'Purple Dome' compete with mum for compactness as well as flower. The lower leaves of this species may brown by midsummer, but any unsightliness is quickly overwhelmed come blooming time. Similar but less prone to legginess are 'Wood's Pink', 'Wood's Blue' and 'Wood's Purple', cultivars of *S. dumosum* (Zone 4). All grow 12–18 in. high and wide.

In taller asters, 'Bluebird' smooth aster (*Symphyotrichum laeve*, Zone 4) shines with blue quarter-sized daisies in 4 ft. sprays. 'Raydon's Favorite' is everyone's favorite, a cultivar of aromatic aster (*S. oblongifolium*, Zone 3) with lavender fall flowers. This pretty but lanky aster is best sheared by half in early summer to keep it to a bushy 3 ft. For something completely different of the aster persuasion, try 'Jindai', a cultivar of Tatarian aster (*Aster tataricus*, Zone 4) with banana-like leaves and straight-arrow stalks of flowers topped with blue daisies at 4 ft.

Astilbe species and cultivars

Astilbe

HARDINESS: Zones 4–8

BLOOM PERIOD: Midsummer

SIZE: 1–3 ft. high, 1–2 ft. wide

H

The feathery princess of flowering plants for shade, astilbe (pron. "ah-STILL-bee") promises tufted, fine-textured paintbrushes in red, pink, purple, and white. All it asks is a mostly shady spot and not-too-dry soil; cultivars of *Astilbe chinensis* are a bit tougher. Besides fine texture, most varieties' tiered symmetrical flowers make for vertical interest as well, and are supported by ferny foliage. For an added foliar show, try red- and purple-leaved 'Delft Lace' and 'Color Flash', or 'Color Flash Lime' for chartreuse.

Astilbe (*Astilbe* cultivar).

Calamintha nepeta and cultivars

Calamint

HARDINESS: Zones 5–10

BLOOM PERIOD: Late summer

SIZE: 1–2 ft. high and wide

H

Calamint comes along like a cool breeze in the dog days of summer, just when the garden needs freshening up. This spreading perennial stretches its minty arms out from a central clump, in and among neighboring plants, before reaching skyward to bloom with millions of tiny white bells. Seedlings may appear if it's happy. Try 'White Cloud' for heaviest bloom, or 'Blue Cloud' if lavender is more your kind of color.

Calamint (*Calamintha nepeta*).

Ceratostigma plumbaginoides

Plumbago

HARDINESS: Zones 5–9

BLOOM PERIOD: Late summer, fall

SIZE: 6–12 in. high, 12–18 in. wide

H

At first, plumbago may strike you as a good enough groundcover, emerging late spring as a neat, weed-smothering mat. Just wait until late summer, when it explodes in shimmering sapphire flowers, followed by (sometimes overlapping with!) fall foliage in blazing orange-red. It's one of the few perennials valued for fall color. Better yet, plumbago thrives in a range of soils and situations, from damp (not wet) to dry, sun to shade, though shade is best on hot sites.

Plumbago (*Ceratostigma plumbaginoides*).

Chrysanthemum and cultivars

Chrysanthemum

HARDINESS: Zones 3/4/5–9

BLOOM PERIOD: Fall

SIZE: 18–30 in. high and wide

A garden favorite traditionally grown as an annual, mums have become a go-to for quick flower color in fall. Rather than a fling with a temporary mum "meatball" you'll forget to compost until long after the thrill is gone, why not commit to a long-term relationship with an old-fashioned variety? These underused gems are more reliably perennial than their daffy dome-shaped cousins. Varieties include pink daisy 'Clara Curtis' (Zone 5); peachy, hardier 'Sheffield' (Zones 3); ruffled bubblegum 'Emperor of China' (Zone 4); and, for those who prefer their mums to echo fall leaves, orange 'Bronze Elegans' (Zone 4).

'Sheffield' chrysanthemum (*Chrysanthemum* 'Sheffield').

Echinacea species and cultivars

Purple coneflower

HARDINESS: Zones 3/5–9

BLOOM PERIOD: Midsummer, late summer

SIZE: 2–3 ft. high and wide

Its common name may be purple, but varieties of popular coneflower come in a raucous array of colors these days, most hardy to Zone 3. The granddaddy of them all, native *Echinacea purpurea*, blooms

Purple coneflower (*Echinacea purpurea* cultivar).

with big pink-purple daisies in summer. At 3 ft., cultivar 'Magnus' grows bigger, while 'Kim's Knee High' is a mini at barely 2 ft. Try 'Tomato Soup' for a volcanic red, or 'White Swan' for a frostier hue. Fluffy double-flowered varieties like white *E*. 'Milkshake' (Zone 5) make great mum alternatives. All coneflowers are best planted in spring in average to dry, well-drained soil, allowing their roots a full growing season to settle in—otherwise, they may have disappeared come the next spring.

'Milkshake' coneflower (*Echinacea* 'Milkshake').

Echinops species and cultivars

Globe thistle

HARDINESS: Zones 3–8

BLOOM PERIOD: Midsummer, late summer

SIZE: 2–4 ft. high, 1–2 ft. wide

H

Got a soft spot for spheres? This thistle is the plant for you. First, its silvery, crenellated foliage emerges, an architectural element in itself. It's quickly followed by flowering stems topped with pointy globes that travel up, up, up as they turn from silver to white or blue. Globe thistle asks for only sun and lean, average to dry soil. It grows a deep taproot, so plant in a spot where it can settle in.

Globe thistle (*Echinops ritro*).

Eupatorium species and cultivars

Joe Pye weed, snakeroot

HARDINESS: Zones 3/4–9

BLOOM PERIOD: Late summer

SIZE: 3–7 ft. high, 2–4 ft. wide

H

A common sight on wetland sites in the Northeast, native Joe Pye weed (*Eupatorium purpureum* and subspecies, like *E. purpureum* subsp. *maculatum*, Zone 3) is like garden phlox writ large, its giant rose-colored cones of flower topping out at a whopping 7 ft. in sun and wet soil. Similar, smaller *E. dubium* 'Little Joe' matures to a more amenable 4 ft., and proves adaptable to moderately dry soil as well. Both grow best in full sun, and bigger Joe may get floppy in excess shade. You may see these plants sold under the genera *Eutrochium* or *Eupatoriadelphus*.

On the other end of the spectrum is 'Chocolate' snakeroot (*Eupatorium rugosum* 'Chocolate', Zone 4), a popular cultivar of another native grown for its fascinating purple foliage as much as its fluffy white flowers. It may grow to 5 ft., but typically tops out shorter, and prefers part sun to part shade. It's also sold as *Ageratina altissima* 'Chocolate'.

'Chocolate' snakeroot (*Eupatorium rugosum* 'Chocolate').

Joe Pye weed (*Eupatorium purpureum*).

Gaillardia species and cultivars

Blanket flower

HARDINESS: Zones 3/4/5–9

BLOOM PERIOD: Midsummer, late summer, fall

SIZE: 1–3 ft. high and wide

If, in summer, you find yourself in search of the antidote to all those spring pastels, blanket flower should be the first plant you try. This native's cultivars bloom with crazy daisies in the hottest colors imaginable—usually some combo of reds and golds, as in 'Arizona Sun' (Zone 3). The 'Gallo' series (Zone 5) burns especially bright, with bicolors and solids, like apricot 'Gallo Peach'. Blanket flower is easy in sun and well-drained soil.

Blanket flower (*Gaillardia* cultivar).

Helenium species and cultivars

Helenium

HARDINESS: Zones 3/4–8

BLOOM PERIOD: Midsummer, late summer, fall

SIZE: 2–3 ft. high, 1–2 ft. wide

Helenium belongs to a group of hot-flowered perennials that punctuate our horticultural memories of the hot summer months. This small perennial blooms with bunches of simple daisies, each like a bouquet of its own, in shades of russet red to orange to gold. Burnt umber 'Moerheim Beauty' (Zone 3) and multicolored 'Mardi Gras' (Zone 4) are two popular cultivars. Helenium prefers average to moist soil, and can be chopped back in late spring to encourage bushiness, though red cultivar 'Ruby Tuesday' reportedly stays compact. All are cultivars of hybrids between species native to the Northeast or further afield in North America.

Helenium (*Helenium* cultivar).

Helianthus species and cultivars

Sunflower

HARDINESS: Zones 4/6–9

BLOOM PERIOD: Late summer, fall

SIZE: 6–10 in. high, 6–36 in. wide

We all know the beloved annual sunflowers, which appear under "Warm-Season Annuals" (page 169), but what about a sunflower that returns year after year? Such sunflowers exist, and better yet, they're tough native plants that make fabulous vertical accents when not in bloom. Willowleaf sunflower (*Helianthus salicifolius*) rises from the ground with symmetrically whirling towers of fine-textured, lime-green foliage, while Maximilian sunflower (*H. maximiliani*) produces a column of more customary dark green sunflower leaves. In sun, both can reach upwards of 10 ft., and bloom in glorious late summer gold. If 10 is a few feet too tall for your garden, try *H. salicifolius* 'First Light' (Zone 6), a flowering phenom at 4–5 ft., or hybrid 'Lemon Queen', a 6-ft. serenade in soft yellow.

Perennial sunflower (*Helianthus* cultivar).

Hemerocallis species and cultivars

Daylily

HARDINESS: Zones 3–9

BLOOM PERIOD: Midsummer, late summer

SIZE: 1–5 ft. high, 1–3 ft. wide

One of the easiest, most popular perennials of all, daylily delights with summer trumpets in a crayon box of hues. Sun and average to moist, rich soil is best for flowers, and for fresh foliage when it's not in bloom, but daylily puts on a worthy show in tough soil and shade, too. Divide clumps if they become crowded and flower less.

Cultivars come in a staggering variety of flower color (all but blue), size (dwarf to large), and even fragrance and rebloom. 'Charles Johnston' blooms gold-throated red, 'Chorus Line' ruffled pink, 'Prairie Blue Eyes' in lavender. Old-fashioned 'Hyperion' flowers fragrant lemon yellow, but similar *Hemerocallis lilioasphodelus* may be most fragrant of all. Standby 'Autumn Minaret' signals the start of that season with yellow-orange flowers held high at 5 ft. Daylily isn't known for interesting foliage—for that, try white-edged *H. fulva* 'Kwanso Variegata'.

'Chicago Apache' daylily (*Hemerocallis* 'Chicago Apache').

Hibiscus species and cultivars

Hibiscus

HARDINESS: Zones 4–9

BLOOM PERIOD: Midsummer, late summer

SIZE: 2–5 ft. high, 2–4 ft. wide

H

If you like to pretend you live in the tropics in the humidity of the northeastern summer, then giant-flowered perennial varieties of hibiscus are a must for your garden. These blousy beauties belie the fact that cold ever visits our climate, and what's more, many are varieties of native *Hibiscus moscheutos*, and flower in pink, red, and white. Look for the popular 'Disco Belle' series in all three colors, or try hybrids 'Kopper King' or 'Plum Crazy' for fab purple foliage, too. Sturdy, shrubby hybrid 'Blue River II' blooms purest white. Perennial hibiscus prefers sun and average to moist soil—even wet—and doesn't do drought.

Hibiscus (*Hibiscus moscheutos* cultivar).

Kirengeshoma palmata

Yellow wax bells

HARDINESS: Zones 5–8

BLOOM PERIOD: Late summer, fall

SIZE: 3–4 ft. high, 2–3 ft. wide

H

This hydrangea cousin grows to shrubby stature and boasts palm-sized, pseudotropical foliage, topped off by yellow spikes of flower akin to foxglove in fall. Wax bells is easy in woodland shade and average to moist soil, and makes a bold textural accent during the growing season for cold-climate gardens.

Yellow wax bells (*Kirengeshoma palmata*).

Liatris species and cultivars

Blazing star

HARDINESS: Zones 3–9

BLOOM PERIOD: Midsummer, late summer

SIZE: 2–5 ft. high, 1–2 ft. wide

Tall pink spikes of fuzzy flowers typify this terrifically vertical plant. A denizen of prairies, species of native blazing star grow easily in sun, much to the delight of butterflies for miles around. The blazing star you'll find for sale most is *Liatris spicata*, which matures to 3–4 ft. high and comes in a few cultivars, like shorter 'Kobold'—2–3 ft., and more likely to stand straight and narrow—and white 'Alba', if pink isn't your thing. For height, try *L. pycnostachya*, a stunner at 5 ft.

Blazing star (*Liatris spicata*).

Lobelia species and cultivars

Lobelia

HARDINESS: Zones 3/4–8

BLOOM PERIOD: Midsummer, late summer

SIZE: 1–4 ft. high, 1–2 ft. wide

A boon to butterflies and hummingbirds, lobelia blooms with tall spires in summer. Two types are common: blue-flowered *Lobelia siphilitica* (Zone 4), and brilliant red *L. cardinalis* (Zone 3), which also goes by the name cardinal flower. Lobelia can sometimes be short-lived, but tends to reseed generously regardless. For flower power and foliage wow factor, try cardinal cultivar 'Black Truffle' with season-long purple leaves. Lobelia is particularly at home in wet places.

Lobelia (*Lobelia cardinalis*).

Monarda species and cultivars

Bee balm

HARDINESS: Zones 4–9

BLOOM PERIOD: Midsummer, late summer

SIZE: 2–5 ft. high, 1–3 ft. wide

Bee balm blooms with architectural pinwheels arrayed in levels up its stems, comes in a number of colors, and as its common name suggests, makes a splash among pollinators of all stripes. Plant bee balm in a sunny spot with well-drained soil and good air circulation to guard against powdery mildew—otherwise, it's an easy plant for summer color. Most bee balm you'll find are cultivars of *Monarda didyma*, like tall, tantalizing 'Jacob Cline', a powerhouse in red at 5 ft.; or 'Marshall's Delight', a more polite height at 3 ft., and pretty in pink. Shorter spotted bee balm (*M. punctata*, 2 ft.) ponies up with odd pink-to-white flowers that look like stars on skewers.

'Jacob Kline' bee balm (*Monarda didyma* 'Jacob Kline').

Origanum species and cultivars

Oregano

HARDINESS: Zones 5–9

BLOOM PERIOD: Midsummer, late summer

SIZE: 12–18 in. high and wide

Oregano isn't just for your kitchen anymore. Though culinary oregano can be ornamental in itself, a couple of varieties of oregano make outstanding groundcovers, just for looks. (They smell great, too.) Blue-leaved *Origanum* ×*laevigatum* 'Pilgrim' blooms in a gradient from light pink to magenta in summer. Hybrid 'Rosenkuppel' flowers a deeper pink, with flowers like tiny drumsticks. Ornamental oregano is easy in average to dry, well-drained soil, and smothers weeds like a champ.

'Pilgrim' ornamental oregano (*Origanum* ×*laevigatum* 'Pilgrim').

Perovskia atriplicifolia and cultivars

Russian sage

HARDINESS: Zones 5–9

BLOOM PERIOD: Midsummer, late summer, fall

SIZE: 3–5 ft. high, 2–4 ft. wide

Like a giant lavender on steroids, Russian sage puts on plumes of lavender above silver foliage in late summer. This taller, shrubby perennial adores no less than blasting sun and lean, dry, alkaline soil—a surefire solution for a shrub-sized presence on sites that bake in summer. Cut this plant to the ground in late winter, before it leafs out, to keep it tidy.

Russian sage (*Perovskia atriplicifolia*).

Persicaria species and cultivars

Fleece flower

HARDINESS: Zones 4–8

BLOOM PERIOD: Midsummer, late summer, fall

SIZE: 2–5 ft. high and wide

Almost every member of the dynamic fleece flower clan described here lays claim both to interesting foliage and beautiful flowers over a very long season, but they're at their best from midsummer to fall. All are easy in sun and average to moist, well-drained soil.

If it's a big, tropical presence you're looking for, try giant fleece flower (*Persicaria polymorpha*), a stunner with beefy foliage and white summer flowers that fade slowly to rose pink. Another favorite, more for foliage, is 'Red Dragon' fleece flower (*P. microcepahala* 'Red Dragon'), a shorter plant with pointy purple leaves arrayed with a chevron pattern.

Giant fleece flower (*Persicaria polymorpha*).

These two make for big but polite clumpers in the garden, while some of their garden-worthy cousins may seed around a bit when conditions are right. *Persicaria virginiana* 'Lance Corporal' is another chevron-patterned beauty that happens to thrive even in dry shade. Cultivar 'Painter's Palette' is similar, but with wild white-splattered variegation. These are cultivars of a native plant—Asian *P. amplexicaulis*, on the other hand, much prefers sun, and comes in a number of color cultivars: red-flowered 'Firetail', white 'Alba', and 'Golden Arrow', a pink-blooming beauty with raucous chartreuse foliage. While you may find a few seedlings of these in your garden, they're not invasive like their cousin Japanese knotweed (*Polygonum tricuspidata*), a rightfully reviled plant impossible to eradicate in the landscape. It lives on another branch of the family tree—don't let a troublesome cousin turn you off to the entire clan.

'Red Dragon' fleece flower (*Persicaria microcephala* 'Red Dragon').

Phlox paniculata cultivars

Garden phlox

HARDINESS: Zones 3–8

BLOOM PERIOD: Midsummer, late summer

SIZE: 2–4 ft. high, 1–3 ft. wide

H

A far cry from its groundcovering cousins, which you'll find in the Early to Midsummer chapter, garden phlox heralds summer with tall drumsticks of fragrant flowers. Alas, this plant is often plagued by powdery mildew, but it's worth seeking out mildew-resistant varieties. White-flowering 'David' is always recommended. Plant in a spot with full sun, well-drained soil, and good air circulation.

Garden phlox (*Phlox paniculata* cultivar).

Rudbeckia species and cultivars

Black-eyed Susan, coneflower

HARDINESS: Zones 3/4–9

BLOOM PERIOD: Midsummer, late summer

SIZE: 2–7 ft. high, 1–4 ft. wide

H

Black-eyed Susan's big, bold, golden daisies are an unmistakable sign summer is at its peak. Also called coneflower, this cheerful native plant is easy to grow, thriving even in part shade. Zone 3–hardy *Rudbeckia fulgida* var. *sullivantii* 'Goldsturm' is most popular. For a Susan of a different stripe, check out *R. maxima*, or giant coneflower (Zone 4). This prairie native sports paddle-shaped blue leaves and single flowers at 7 ft. tall. They fade quickly, but its brown seedheads are a favorite of acrobatic birds. Give giant coneflower full sun to guard against flopping. Another tall coneflower is long-blooming *R. laciniata* 'Herbstsonne' (Zone 5). If you're looking for something unique but don't fancy a coneflower taller than you, try *R. subtomentosa* 'Henry Eilers' (Zone 4), a cultivar whose curled golden petals look like bicycle spokes.

Black-eyed Susan (*Rudbeckia fulgida* var. *sullivantii* 'Goldsturm').

'Herbstsonne' coneflower (*Rudbeckia laciniata* 'Herbstsonne').

Sidalcea 'Party Girl'

Checker mallow

HARDINESS: Zones 5–7

BLOOM PERIOD: Midsummer

SIZE: 2–3 ft. high, 1–2 ft. wide

H

You may know hollyhocks as classics in the cottage garden, and indeed, these biennials have always been popular for their towers of hibiscus-like blooms. If you're in the market for something similar and more long-lived, try this mini-hollyhock, an easy plant for a splash of vertical color. Cultivar 'Party Girl' makes her debutante debut in summer pink. Give checker mallow sun and average soil, and it's off like a shot.

'Party Girl' checker mallow (*Sidalcea* 'Party Girl').

Solidago species and cultivars

Goldenrod

HARDINESS: Zones 3–9

BLOOM PERIOD: Late summer, fall

SIZE: 2–4 ft. high and wide

H

Yes, you might be sneezing when you see goldenrod in bloom, but don't blame this plant—in fact, its pollen is too large to even reach your schnozz. The real culprit is ragweed (*Ambrosia* species), which blooms at the same time and is far less conspicuous, leaving its gorgeous gold cousin to shoulder the blame. Goldenrod is a snap to grow in sun, and comes in a number of great cultivars. Architectural *Solidago rugosa* 'Fireworks' blooms with loose sprays of canary, while newer, smaller hybrid 'Little Lemon' flowers a pale citron. All are native, and all promise a world of pollinators for your flowerbed.

'Little Lemon' goldenrod (*Solidago* 'Little Lemon').

Tricyrtis formosana and cultivars, *T. hirta* and cultivars

Toad lily

HARDINESS: Zones 4–8

BLOOM PERIOD: Late summer

SIZE: 1–3 ft. high, 1–2 ft. wide

H ◐ ● 🌡

Toad lily's common name doesn't begin to do justice to this all-star for shade. It begins the season looking much like Solomon's seal (*Polygonatum* species), with tiers of dark green arranged like ladders up arching stems. Its flowers, on the other hand, set it apart: odd, waxy starbursts of bloom in a battery of colors, many speckled erratically with a contrasting hue. Toad lily thrives in shady conditions and average to moist soil.

Toad lily (*Tricyrtis formosana* cultivar).

Verbascum species and cultivars

Mullein

HARDINESS: Zones 5–10

BLOOM PERIOD: Midsummer, late summer

SIZE: 2–8 ft. high, 1–3 ft. wide

H ☀ ≡ 🦌

Mullein (*Verbascum* cultivar).

The tall spires of mullein (pron. "mullen") make vertical exclamation points in the garden. Some make bold statements, like monumental Greek mullein (*Verbascum olympicum*), a tower of acid yellow at 10 ft. Others are more quietly exclamatory, like woolly leaved, buttery *V. chaixii*, and serve equally well as foliage plants. Another favorite, *V.* 'Southern Charm' flowers pink, and reblooms if sheered back to its basal leaves after the first round. Tough, drought-resistant mullein does best in sun, and while many may be biennial—growing their first year, blooming the second—they typically reseed, so you'll have mini-mullein to spare the year after.

Veronicastrum virginicum and cultivars

Culver's root

HARDINESS: Zones 3–8

BLOOM PERIOD: Midsummer, late summer

SIZE: 4–7 ft. high, 2–4 ft. wide

Native culver's root is a feast of botanical architecture, and a must as a vertical accent. This plant flowers late summer with scores of fuzzy pipe cleaner candelabra, perched carefully at the tippy-top of tall stems, each arrayed with symmetrical tiers of leaves. Culver's root is a cinch to grow in sun and average to moist (even wet) soil. The species blooms white, but colorful light purple cultivars 'Lavender Towers' and 'Fascination' make a worthy showing, too.

Culver's root (*Veronicastrum virginicum*).

WINTER

Horticultural Coda

Winter in the Northeast is when the garden and we, as gardeners, rest. Like it or not, winter is the coda of seasons—a chance to stop and regroup before beginning again. Fortunately, the winter landscape isn't without its charms. Besides the plants in this chapter, many multiseason plants shine brightly in the winter garden. (See the Framework chapter.) Think about the winter window you find yourself sitting by most, or the path you most travel, and consider these plants accordingly.

TREES AND SHRUBS

Cornus species and cultivars

Osier dogwood

HARDINESS: Zones 3–8

SIZE: 5–6 ft. high and wide

D

Dogwood comes in two sizes, tree and shrub, and while tree-sized dogwoods really do their thing in summer and spring, shrubby osier dogwood shines most in winter. That's because this dogwood's branches come in a lava flow of red, orange, and yellow that set the winter landscape alight. Red twig dogwood is most common, and that common name is given to a few popular species and their cultivars, most notably native *Cornus sericea*. Gaining in popularity are yellow twig varieties like 'Flaviramea' and 'Budd's Yellow', and a wild red-orange cultivar called *C. sanguinea* 'Midwinter Fire'. New branches

'Midwinter Fire' osier dogwood (*Cornus sanguinea* 'Midwinter Fire').

Bearsfoot hellebore (*Helleborus foetidus*) flowers in winter.

are most showy, so brutal pruning is a must—don't be afraid to cut a quarter of osier dogwood's oldest stems to the ground in late winter, before it leafs out. This plant blooms with fuzzy white flowers in summer, but it's grown for its winter stems, and is typically less exciting during the growing season. Look for variegated cultivars like *C. alba* 'Ivory Halo' in red twig and *C. sericea* 'Silver and Gold' in yellow for interest that's nearly year-round.

Corylus avellana 'Contorta', 'Red Majestic'

Contorted filbert

HARDINESS: Zones 4–8

SIZE: 8–10 ft. high and wide

D

Winter reveals what contorted filbert's leaves keep hidden most of the growing season—irregular branches that twist and undulate outward in a most spectacular fashion. If there ever was a shrub made for winter, this is it. Contorted filbert, also called Harry Lauder's walking stick, is easy in average conditions and soil. Keep an eye out for uncontorted suckers at ground level that you'll need to prune out, and don't be alarmed if its leaves begin to contort as well. 'Red Majestic' is a double whammy, with contorted form in winter, and gorgeous red-purple leaves in season that fade gently to green.

Contorted filbert (*Corylus avellana* 'Contorta').

Hamamelis species and cultivars

Witch hazel

HARDINESS: Zones 3/5–9

BLOOM PERIOD: Midwinter, late winter

SIZE: 8–15 ft. high and wide

D ☀ ◐ ◑ ≡ 🦌 📍

The must-have shrub for any winter garden, witch hazel proves gorgeous flower and fragrance need not wait 'til spring. This plant's frizzy, spidery flowers in yellow, orange, red, and coral dot its branches at neat intervals, and often perfume the chilly air with their spicy scent. Witch hazel's vase shape makes it an elegant addition in form throughout the year as well. Fans of yellow should check out *Hamamelis* ×*intermedia* 'Arnold Promise', while 'Jelena' dazzles in orange, 'Diane' in red. These are hybrid cultivars of Asian species and hardy to Zone 5, but those further north strike gold with Zone 3–hardy native *H. virginiana*.

Witch hazel (*Hamamelis* cultivar).

Witch hazel (*Hamamelis* cultivar).

Ilex verticillata and cultivars

Winterberry

HARDINESS: Zones 3–9

SIZE: 3–10 ft. high and wide

D

Though its evergreen cousins may live in the Framework chapter, winterberry (*Ilex verticillata*) doesn't truly come into its own until that freezing season. Its thornless leaves are a sumptuous hunter green, but when they drop in late fall this holly brings its "A" game. Female plants make a riot of red berries so hot they're sure to stop traffic, and well into winter. A boon for overwintering birds, its cultivars also come in gold and coral. Winterberry thrives in wet soil and makes a great shrubby addition to bog gardens, but adapts to average sites too. Male and female plants are a must for fruit.

Winterberry (*Ilex verticillata*).

Salix 'Golden Curls', 'Scarlet Curls', *S. matsudana* 'Tortuosa'

Corkscrew willow

HARDINESS: Zones 4/5–8

SIZE: 20–30 ft. high, 10–15 ft. wide

D

This willow looks much like any other during the growing season until closer inspection, when you'll notice its intricately curled branches—an astounding sight in the winter landscape. *Salix matsudana* 'Tortuosa' (Zone 5) has green foliage and brown bark. Better yet, hybrids 'Scarlet Curls' and 'Golden Curls' (Zone 4) promise red and yellow twigs, respectively, a terrific foil for snow in winter. All can be trained into trees or pruned hard in late winter to keep them shrubby.

'Golden Curls' corkscrew willow (*Salix* 'Golden Curls').

Poncirus trifoliata and cultivars

Hardy orange

HARDINESS: Zones 5–9

BLOOM PERIOD: Late spring, early summer

SIZE: 8–20 ft. high, 5–15 ft. wide

D

Hardy orange is a plant of many charms, but I'm betting its gigantic thorns might not have made your list. In winter, however, those exquisite spines and odd green stems are a welcome sight against a backdrop of snow. Mature plants add orange fruit to the mix, but it's much better left as winter decoration than picked to eat. Hardy orange blooms early summer, with white flowers of variable fragrance, but shop for a plant in bloom if it's that citrus scent you crave. Hardy orange is a bulletproof plant in sun to part shade. Cultivar 'Flying Dragon' makes for even more winter interest, with all this plus contorted branches.

Hardy orange (*Poncirus trifoliata*).

PERENNIALS AND BULBS

Crocus species and cultivars

Crocus

HARDINESS: Zones 3–8

BLOOM PERIOD: Late winter

SIZE: 4–6 in. high and wide

Long before the party girls of the bulb world take the stage in spring, crocus pushes its way through snow to bloom spectacularly in spite of freezing weather. Glowing clumps of this easy plant flower in shades of blue to lavender and purple to white and yellow, and go dormant by midspring. Plant crocus 2–3 in. deep and 3–4 in. apart in fall, and beware of squirrels, who adore freshly dug crocus corms. Overlay ground above new plants with chicken wire to protect them, or go with a rodent-resistant variety like *Crocus tommasianus*.

Eranthis hyemalis

Winter aconite

HARDINESS: Zones 3–7

BLOOM PERIOD: Late winter

SIZE: 4–6 in. high and wide

Canary yellow isn't a color we associate with winter, but yellow is where it's at with winter aconite, and just at the point near winter's end when we gardeners find ourselves maniacally impatient. This little ephemeral goes dormant by late spring, and does best in average to moist, well-drained soil, on sites that are sunny when it blooms and shadier later on—deciduous woodlands work well. It's best planted as a dormant tuber from late summer to early fall, and you're advised to soak tubers overnight prior to planting.

Crocus (*Crocus* cultivars). RIGHT **Winter aconite (*Eranthis hyemalis*).**

Galanthus nivalis and cultivars

Snowdrop

HARDINESS: Zones 3–7

BLOOM PERIOD: Midwinter, late winter

SIZE: 6–8 in. high, 4–6 in. wide

Snowdrop is the first plant out of the gate, year after year, with flocks of tiny, china-white flowers like birds on the wing. Earlier than even crocus, this little bulb's subtlety in the quiet of the winter landscape is its strong suit. Snowdrops work best in drifts, great in lawns or woodlands. Be sure to let their foliage yellow before mowing in spring.

Snowdrop (*Galanthus nivalis*).

Helleborus species and cultivars

Hellebore

HARDINESS: Zones 4/5–9

BLOOM PERIOD: Midwinter, late winter

SIZE: 12–18 in. high and wide

While a number of Framework perennials contribute to winter interest, one die-hard saves its seasonal display for winter: hellebore, or Lenten rose. This tough plant sports leathery leaves and delicate, bowl-shaped flowers that seem to be lit from within, in a complex mix of shades from purple, pink, and rose, to white, yellow, and near green. In mild winters with little snow cover, they may begin to bloom midwinter.

Hellebores thrive in partial to full shade, though they'll take more sun in winter, and do well in dry shade under deciduous trees. You'll likely find hybrids and cultivars of *Helleborus orientalis* or *H.* ×*hybridus* in a rainbow of colors. Species bearsfoot hellebore (*H. foetidus*, Zone 5) features finely cut foliage like mini palm fronds, a far cry from the snowy climes where it thrives.

Hellebore (*Helleborus* cultivars).

DESIGN

Building Blocks for Every Landscape

As much as you plant, as well as you know the seasons, and as seasoned a gardener as you may be, if you know a thing or two about design, you're more likely to be inspired by your garden. Take a look at the elements and principles of garden design here, see how they apply to the gardens that follow, and consider how they're at play in your landscape. You might be surprised to discover what better design can do for you.

A lively vignette at Chanticleer Garden in Wayne, Pennsylvania.

FUNDAMENTAL DETAILS

Your Sensory Toolbox

The secret to building a landscape is simple: it's all in the details. It helps to think of your yard as a giant 3-D puzzle. Don't let solving it intimidate you! This is one puzzle you get to plan yourself. The raw materials with which you'll fashion the pieces of your puzzle, and the qualities of those materials, are called *elements of design*. The organizing *principles of design* serve as the dovetails and connecting joints you'll use to bind the pieces of your puzzle together. Together, these details are what you'll use to make your landscape a cohesive, finished whole.

ELEMENTS

Space is what everything you're looking at inhabits. In landscape design, the area taken up by all the stuff that fills space—plants, a fence, your house—is called positive space. The open air that surrounds all that stuff is called negative space. Positive and negative space have a yin-yang relationship, and can affect how you feel in subtle ways. Lots of positive space in your garden's composition makes it feel active, dynamic, a place where things happen. It can also make your garden feel cluttered and claustrophobic. More negative space could make your garden feel meditative and zen-like—too much, and it could feel empty.

Line is the word for where things meet—say, where a tree meets the sky, or where your flowerbed meets your lawn. You can use line to do things like lead the eye in a specific direction, and make a space feel bigger or smaller. Straight lines create structure, evoke a sense of formality, and can be used for major emphasis at the specific point where they end. Curved lines feel more organic, relaxed, and even mysterious when they curve around out of view. Horizontal lines bring your eye down, while vertical lines draw your attention skyward. Extended horizontal or vertical line can make a space feel larger.

A many and varied mix of plants in the garden of Ellen Lathi, Needham, Massachusetts.

Form happens when a group of lines come together to create a shape, and the term "form" refers to both the two-dimensional outline of that shape (the rectangular face of a bluestone tile, for example) and the three-dimensional outline (a tree that's rounded on top, like a big, leafy ball on a trunk). Geometric shapes with clearly lined edges, such as rectangles and circles, bring formality to landscape design. The naturalistic shape of many plants feels more casual and organic. Trees and shrubs are often discussed in terms of their 3-D form: rounded, weeping, pyramidal, oval, columnar, and vase.

Texture, subtle and evocative, is one of those omnipresent qualities in a landscape that you may register unconsciously, but it shapes your sense of place all the more for it. In landscape design, texture usually refers to a few things. One is sheen: if something glints, mirror-like, in the light, we call it glossy. If it looks velvety to the touch, it's soft. Glassy surfaces are called smooth, while those that appear rough or jagged are coarse. If a plant's leaves are big and bawdy, we call its texture bold, while those with many tiny leaves are fine in texture, and those in between are medium.

Color. If you've ever taken a basic art class, you know the color wheel, and its principles apply here, too. Colors that appear next to each other on the wheel are analogous colors, and designing with an analogous palette makes a space feel more serene. Those that face each other across the wheel are complementary, and these colors are best used together to create more vibrant compositions. If your scheme uses a single color for effect, we call it monochromatic. It's also important to talk about color in terms of "temperature": red, orange, and yellow are considered hot colors; green, blue, and violet are cool colors. Hot equals energy, while cool equals calm, but there are many combinations in between. Also, pale colors serve to link saturated colors together, and show up better in low light. Dark colors recede. Saturated shades read best in sun, although the brightest will shine most when weather is cloudy, or in light shade—otherwise, an electric color in sun can be downright neon.

Ephemeral qualities, a whole host of harder-to-pin-down features, combine with the other design elements to create a sense of place in the landscape. The biggest is context. Remember the discussion on geography? Consider whether your garden's setting (or pieces of it) are coastal, metropolitan, woodland, mountain, wetland, or meadow, and you've got your context. Think about the four seasons, too, and how your garden changes with those seasons over the course of the year. Also consider how light moves through your garden over the course of the day at different times of year. Things like this that change with time are often called temporal qualities. Movement is another ephemeral design element, one that makes spaces feel more lively. Sound can have the same effect if it's loud or stirring, as with a group of busy birds—or it can create serenity, as with a burbling fountain. Finally, when it comes to landscapes, fragrance is a quality that should never be underestimated in creating a sense of place.

PRINCIPLES

Harmony is the ultimate design goal for any garden composition. Sometimes called unity, harmony happens when everything in the landscape knits together to form a cohesive whole. In a harmonious garden, you'll feel as though everything is in its place. Simple enough, but tricky to achieve! You can encourage harmony through repetition of specific design elements, like a color, either literally or by echoing that element from one garden vignette to the next. This creates rhythm. On a smaller scale, similar elements can also be arranged together—usually in an odd number, because the eye typically sees an odd numbers of elements as more linked than an even number—to create a unified group.

Order, simply put, is the way you arrange everything in your garden. Imagine you're setting a table, and you know where each serving piece should go in each setting. Design works the same way, except, of course, you get to decide how to organize the elements of your design to achieve harmony. There will probably be a pecking order among the pieces of your design: which stands out most? Which are supporting players? This is called hierarchy.

Balance fits within order, and refers to a specific way things in your landscape compare to other things. We know the landscape is made up of lines, right? If you imagine the line of a path, balance can be symmetrical, meaning there are two or more matching elements in corresponding spots on either side of that path, mirroring each other. Balance can also be asymmetrical, which means those elements don't match.

Scale and proportion. How big or small are the pieces of your garden? That's their scale. Now, how big or small are those pieces compared to other pieces? That's proportion. These two principles go hand in hand, because it's vital not only to consider the size of different elements, but also how they size up with their neighbors. After all, a 10-ft. shrub may dominate your border and all the plants around it, but it may look teeny if your border abuts a three-story mansion.

Focus is when you use a specific element that stands out from all the others so it draws the eye. It could be the curving end of an otherwise linear path, or a colorful object calling out for attention. The thing that actually draws your eye is called a focal point. Focus can also be diffuse, such that elements in a tableau blend together.

Simplicity and variety, another principle pair, work together to achieve balance and harmony. Simplicity refers to how much of the same element you use in your garden, and variety is how much you drop in elements that don't match the others. All simplicity and no variety can make a garden dull indeed—on the other hand, a garden with one or two each of a hundred plants can feel haphazard. Simplicity and variety work in tandem to keep things poised but interesting.

The geometric wire sphere juxtaposed with the naturalistic forms of the plants is a classic example of contrast in form. Morning light and fog are both ephemeral, as is the way they interact with this planting.

CASE STUDIES

Design in Action in Seven Northeast Gardens

Though we may be able to define elements and principles of design, the ways in which they can be utilized in the landscape are vast, and as individual as gardeners themselves. The following examples are intended to help you discover how to put design into practice in your garden.

HUDSON VALLEY

Millerton, New York
OWNERS: Jack Hyland and Larry Wente

Carved out of farmland in the hills of New York's Hudson Valley, this garden pays homage to its pastoral roots with scores of flowing grasses and other meadow plants organized along a central axis. The pair of gardeners who built it work within a typical meadow setting, and their garden is a stunning study in contrasts: modern and traditional, formal and informal, subtle and bold.

OPPOSITE Color cascades from violet vines in the background to red, gold, chartreuse, and finally a restful green. Form does the same, from tall and upright to mounded to the punctuation mark of the potted banana (*Ensete ventricosum* 'Maurellii'). All come together to create harmony in an early morning fog.

RIGHT Large-scale containers filled with *Canna* similar in proportion to the front door create a sense of drama, which, in turn, alludes to a dramatic view opposite the door.

TOP This garden is arranged along an axis, a line that stretches out from the house. Features and plants are arrayed on either side of this axis. The house and vertical plantings run perpendicular to the axis's line. Grasses always add the ephemeral quality of movement to any vignette. BOTTOM Everything in the garden is ordered around its central axis. Upright trellises and arborvitae (*Thuja* 'Degroot's Spire') set the tone in height, a step lower from the house, followed by grasses and hedges of various heights. This garden is also a perfect example of symmetrical balance.

Grasses are fine texture personified. A well-placed New Zealand flax (*Phormium*) adds a dash of bold. A mostly grasses planting also equals simplicity in texture and shape. Even the New Zealand flax is similar in shape. This planting's variety lies in its colors.

SOUTHEAST VERMONT

Putney, Vermont
OWNERS: **Gordon and Mary Hayward**

This garden sits in the hills of southern Vermont, where pasture mingles with meadow, all on the site of woodlands of yesteryear. Many mature trees remain. Its proprietors divide the garden by rooms, each with a different flavor, but with a consistency of style that easily blends one into the next.

'Gold Heart' bleeding heart (*Dicentra* 'Gold Heart') steals the focus in this tableau. The careful interplay of color and texture, as well as natural, botanical, and man-made forms, come together to make a harmonious vignette.

Asymmetrical balance is on display in a curving path bounded by formal hedging at left, and informal, natural plants at right (like blooming *Kalmia* and *Leucothoe*), as well as the red urn.

Columns made from old honeylocust trees (*Gleditsia*) represent upright, geometrical form in a naturalistic package. They're softened by the more free-flowing form of the plants at their feet.

TOP Negative and positive space are clearly delineated here, respectively, in the open space of the path and the tall plantings that rise on either side of it. BOTTOM The sound of water soothes even the busiest garden, as does the way light reflects on its surface. Sound is an ephemeral quality in design.

Everything in this garden is ordered in its place—a screen of *Thuja*, veggies and herbs bounded by boxwood (*Buxus*), and an eye-catching structure at center, supported by a terra-cotta urn below.

SEACOAST NEW HAMPSHIRE

Greenland, New Hampshire

Its view of Great Bay—a tidal estuary where the waters of the Piscataqua River meet the Atlantic—give this garden a sought-after setting. The proximity to the bay and the accompanying conditions make it a prime example for coastal and near-coastal gardeners to follow. A garden for flowers first and foremost, its owners prove coastal challenges need not preclude bounty.

The low translucence of this garden is an ephemeral quality that responds to its context next to the flat, translucent surface of Great Bay. This scene offers a wealth of variety in botanical color and form, and it's held together by simplicity in the similarity in scale of these plants.

Saturated colors are linked by pastel peach and plenty of green, while various plant forms mingle in perfect scale to one another, rolling up against the backdrop of trees. All together, they're a study in harmony.

Mounded form is on display here, in the shrubs, as well as the *Clematis* on the trellis.

TOP The lines of daylily (*Hemerocallis fulva*), cattail, and bridge match perfectly, and all run perpendicular to the line of the path. In terms of balance, these elements also create symmetry. BOTTOM Hot colors like red and orange are the order of the day here, but they're subtly tempered by cool blue-greens. A hierarchical order of mounded plant forms topped off by flowers meshes together to create this vignette.

SUBURBAN BOSTON

Needham, Massachusetts
OWNER: **Ellen Lathi**

Proving the suburbs may be the most diverse setting of all, this garden is a blend of metropolitan, wetland, and woodland contexts. Its owner's fondness for foliage means its beauty spans the entire growing season. Her eye for texture, containers, and personal garden ornaments makes it exceptional year-round.

The scale of the red banana (*Ensete ventricosum* 'Maurellii') in this front yard in proportion to the house is a telling sign that you're entering a garden where everything is larger than life.

The close confines of the shade house in this garden respond perfectly to the ephemeral closeness of its woodland context. The line of the path here clearly brings you to the shade house, and is paralleled by lines of groundcover, shrubs, and trees.

Rocks and trees are both naturalistic in form, but the low, rounded form of the stone cairn also creates an interesting contrast beside a forest of vase-shaped river birches (*Betula nigra*).

TOP A scattering of fall leaves, the play of light's reflection on surfaces after the rain, moss growing up the flanks of a concrete canine—these are all examples of ephemeral qualities in the garden. A simple palette of rusty red-browns, chartreuse, and green knit this vignette together, even as the plants and ornaments in it are many and varied. BOTTOM In terms of order, a clear hierarchy exists in this frame of view, from lawn all the way up to trees. Rounded shapes that surround the lawn gradually give way to the trees that point upward with more columnar and pyramidal form.

BERKSHIRE HILLS

Sheffield, Massachusetts
OWNER: **Maria Nation**

Nestled among the granite knuckles of the Berkshires, this garden makes for a fascinating study between formal and informal, traditional and whimsical. The gardener who lives here employs color, shape, and texture to create a theatrical style all her own.

Complements of color and a hierarchy of shapes and textures create a harmonious vignette. Containers of tender plants that have to come in for winter are one example of how gardens can be ephemeral, and change with the seasons.

Vertical form is on display in white-blooming culver's root (*Veronicastrum*) at top and the flanking shrubs, as well as flowers of blue fescue (*Festuca*). These make for great contrast with the rounded plant forms below.

Complementary colors cool blue and bright yellow accentuate this path.

A study in order, a white-flecked dappled willow draws attention through an arbor to a white umbrella and dining set—all with the blessing of the house, also white, and clearly in charge, as evidenced by the bold red of the climbing rose (*Rosa*) that grows up its side.

Bright red *Astilbe* contrasts perfectly with a sea of blue-green leaves below. This planting naturally prompts your eye to follow the sinuous line it guides. An upright *Ilex* 'Sky Pencil' acts as a signpost along the way.

BROOKLYN

Fort Greene, New York
OWNER: **James Golden**

The most populous city in the United States plays host to this tiny oasis. Short on space but long on tranquility, this garden puts to rest the notion that the two are mutually exclusive. Its creator turns sense of place on its ear: the garden's lushness defies its urban context, but it reflects the city, too, both in arrangement and, quite literally, in the pool at its center.

Even though this garden is small, large-scale plants are key, as they respond to the built environment around them. It's also a good illustration of positive and negative space—the garden inhabits the positive space around the edges and merges with the buildings behind it, while the negative space at its center blends with that of the open air above.

A menagerie of fine- and bold-textured plants provides a study in contrasts, all against the smooth backdrop of the fence.

The changing nature of sunlight through the course of the day and its interaction with the water feature are examples of ephemeral qualities. The garden's balance is roughly symmetrical.

Grasses and sedum (*Sedum* cultivars) that attract busy bees embrace the ephemeral quality of motion, while mountain mint (*Pycnanthemum muticum*) employs scent.

The perfect alchemy of hot and cool color, bold and fine texture, this vignette is a stunning study in harmony.

SUBURBAN PHILADELPHIA

Swarthmore, Pennsylvania
OWNER: **Andrew Bunting**

Proving again that suburbs are full of surprises, this garden features a meadow out front, and a lawn in back that unrolls against a backdrop of mature trees. Studded with annuals and containerized tropicals, it challenges visitors to pause with wonder at every turn, the clear intention of its owner.

Even bold-textured plants soften the stone walls of this house, and their glossy leaves contrast with its matte surface.

The carefully ordered arrangement of every element in this garden marries wild with refined.

TOP In this harmonious group, a quartet of evergreens is fronted by a similar number of forest grass (*Hakonechloa*) plants, backup singers to the chairs on the terrace. A hot red gate looks on, and various warm yellows echo throughout, all enveloped in cool green. BOTTOM Ever ephemeral, the tall blooms of fleece flower (*Persicaria amplexicaulis* 'Firetail'), and stems of threadleaf bluestar (*Amsonia hubrichtii*) are on the move at the slightest breeze. In scale, the height and reach of the plants along this path make it feel like a jungle trek.

Upright stance and big, bold leaves create tropical form in this *Canna*. OPPOSITE An ornate iron gate is a focal point that says "Open me, and see what's inside." The pergola of vines that rises above this gateway creates a vignette that's roughly symmetrical in balance.

PRACTICE

Knowledge for Growing Needs

You've learned a little about the site where your garden grows, surveyed the plants you could grow in it, and found a bit of design inspiration—undoubtedly by now you're ready to get your hands in the dirt. This section is all about just that. We'll look at the Northeast from a plant's viewpoint, learn why great soil grows great gardens, consider the other creatures you'll be gardening with, and touch on key duties of caring for your plants. Ready to put what you've learned into practice? Let's get started.

Containers in the garden of Andrew Bunting, Swarthmore, Pennsylvania.

A "Plant's-Eye View" of the Northeast

There's a very good reason why Environment falls under Practice. Simply, your garden will grow best if you understand and work with its environment. How hot or cold does it get in your garden? What's the soil like, and what other creatures are rooting around in it besides you? The answers to questions like these are important.

HARDINESS ZONES

The first thing to consider when choosing a new plant is its hardiness. Hardiness is a term that describes how low the temperature can drop before a plant dies.

The U.S. Department of Agriculture's Plant Hardiness Zone Map is the most widely accepted resource for figuring out your hardiness zone. The USDA divides the country into 13 zones based on average low temperature, then subdivides each zone into "a" and "b," which allows gardeners to pinpoint within five degrees the average low at their site—"a" being colder, "b" warmer. More often than not, as in this book, plant hardiness is given in whole zones, such as "Zones 6–10." If you're shopping for plants and see this listed on a plant's tag, you'll know this plant has survived winter lows in Zone 6a (–10 to –5 degrees F).

We know the Northeast is incredibly diverse in climate, and according to recent USDA mapping, our region encompasses almost four entire hardiness zones, from Zones 3b to 7b. (In fact, the state of New York alone spans all of these zones.) Given the sheer number of zones in the Northeast and the nuances of their borders, printing a detailed zone map in this book would require many pages. A better way to map your zone is to search the internet for "USDA Hardiness Zones," or visit planthardiness.ars.usda.gov. This and other sites allow you to view zones by state, and to find your exact zone by entering your zip code. If you're familiar with your garden site's average low temperature, you can refer to the zone chart here.

Learn your garden from the plants' perspective, and your plants will likely reward you, as in the garden of Maria Nation in Sheffield, Massachusetts.

Zones and temperatures

ZONE	TEMPERATURE (°F)			TEMPERATURE (°C)		
1	−50	AND	BELOW	−45.6	AND	BELOW
2a	−45	TO	−50	−42.8	TO	−45.5
2b	−40	TO	−45	−40.0	TO	−42.7
3a	−35	TO	−40	−37.3	TO	−40.0
3b	−30	TO	−35	−34.5	TO	−37.2
4a	−25	TO	−30	−31.7	TO	−34.4
4b	−20	TO	−25	−28.9	TO	−31.6
5a	−15	TO	−20	−26.2	TO	−28.8
5b	−10	TO	−15	−23.4	TO	−26.1
6a	−5	TO	−10	−20.6	TO	−23.3
6b	0	TO	−5	−17.8	TO	−20.5
7a	5	TO	0	−15.0	TO	−17.7
7b	10	TO	5	−12.3	TO	−15.0
8a	15	TO	10	−9.5	TO	−12.2
8b	20	TO	15	−6.7	TO	−9.4
9a	25	TO	20	−3.9	TO	−6.6
9b	30	TO	25	−1.2	TO	−3.8
10a	35	TO	30	1.6	TO	−1.1
10b	40	TO	35	4.4	TO	1.7
11	40	AND	ABOVE	4.5	AND	ABOVE

Fall foliage of sourwood (*Oxydendrum*).

Climate Change: What Does It Mean for Gardening?

Whether or not you believe global climate change is man-made, the general consensus among today's scientific community and beyond is that it's happening. While the uncertainties are rightly anxiety producing, the public conversation has reached a level of depth that's not just about big picture questions anymore. Sure, you're right to worry about the possibility of extreme weather events—and beyond worrying about large-scale impacts, it's only natural to wonder how the effects of climate change will trickle down to affect smaller things. Your garden, for example. While it's probably safe to say everyone hopes to avoid catastrophes of all kinds, as a gardener in a changing climate, you can depend on a few realities:

Warmer winters are bound to happen if the globe warms. It's important to check your hardiness zone on the current USDA Plant Hardiness Map; it's been recently updated to include more climate data, and many sites have already shifted slightly to warmer zones. That said, there's always the chance of . . .

Unpredictable weather. It's a hallmark of climate change. While some winters may be a bit warmer, others may dip to cooler levels. Precipitation, another all-important factor for gardeners to consider, may also vary. In the Northeast, this could mean some nearly snowless winters, while others could find us regularly digging out. It could also mean drought during the growing seasons. Plants are cyclical organisms that not only rely on factors like temperature and precipitation to grow, they also rely on these factors to know when to grow and how much, and when to do things like bloom and produce seed.

Extreme weather events are another certainty with climate change. If the Northeast warms, the region will be more prone to hurricanes, as are the Southeast and the tropics. We'll also be more susceptible to tornadoes, drought, and flooding.

The answer to all of these questions is simple: plant tough. Catastrophic weather events aside, the plants in these pages aren't just beautiful—most are workhorses, hardy and happy in a range of zones, and therefore more likely to withstand swings in temperature and precipitation. If sited correctly, many also require fewer inputs (water, fertilizer, and pesticides), which means they're automatically more environmentally friendly to boot.

The future of our climate, much like pondwater, is unclear.

ECOSYSTEMS

Whether or not you're aware of it, when you're in your garden, there's life all around you. It's true! No one gardens in a vacuum, and if you're outdoors, you can be sure you and your plants are surrounded by untold numbers of tiny life forms. Some can be pesky, it's true, but many more than that gladly work alongside you to grow something beautiful. That's the definition of an ecosystem: any community of living things that are all in it together. The actions of each one affect others, and everyone is affected by changes in resources and living situations within the ecosystem. Winter turns to spring, for example, plants begin to grow, and food becomes more available. A tree grows up, casting shade below it where once there was sun. A new home is built—yours or, say, a bird's nest.

The overarching type of ecosystem you live in closely mirrors the type of setting that best describes your garden from the Geography chapter, and your garden functions as a cog in the machine of that larger ecosystem. Understanding that basic concept can not only help you understand how your personal landscape shapes the big picture, it can help you learn how to work within it to make your garden more beautiful, successful, rewarding, and inviting.

MICROCLIMATES

When choosing where a plant will live in your landscape, it's important to think about how conditions may vary from place to place within that landscape, even beyond knowing your hardiness zone. Which areas get more sun, and which get more shade? Which are colder in the winter, and which tend to be more protected? Is there an area that's especially windy or wet? These different areas within any given landscape are called microclimates.

To get to the bottom of your microclimates, figure out which direction is north and go from there. If your garden is completely open, with no barriers, your microclimate should jibe with your hardiness zone. Many of us, on the other hand, plant our gardens around larger obstacles and structures—like trees or fences, but especially houses. If you're planting a garden around your house, here's the rundown on microclimate orientation:

The north side of a house is always cooler and shadier. Prevailing winds in our part of the country tend to be out of the Northwest, so the north side will often be windier as well. In winter, the north side of your house will likely be the coldest. Hardy and shade-loving plants are often well suited to the north side.

The south side, opposite the north, is sun-splashed and sultry. Besides being a boon to sun-loving plants, the south makes a good spot for plants whose hardiness you may question, because warmth is more constant there in winter.

A house's east side is where you'll find gentle morning sun, a favorite of many plants, as it gets them all the rays they need without all the heat. The east side sits in the lee of a house, so it's also a good spot for plants that need a bit of protection from wind—but because of that, soil there can be drier as well. One notable exception occurs during those coastal storms we all know as nor'easters, when weather comes at us from the northeast, rather than the northwest.

The west side of a house is the windward side, bearing the brunt of most wind and precipitation that comes calling, as well as bright, hot afternoon sun.

Given that, the west can be wetter, and tends to work best for heartier, and hardier, plants.

Though fences, hedges, trees and other structures also make for varying degrees of these microclimates, the concepts are much the same. When siting plants around trees, it's important to note that trees consume groundwater, whereas homes don't, so soil conditions will be drier all around. Climate-controlled structures and paved surfaces like driveways also channel heat back into the soil, both from the rays they soak up from the sun and, for homes, from inside, depending on how well they're insulated. Finally, soil moisture and drainage affects microclimates significantly. Cool air tends to drift downward and pool in low spots, making those areas much icier if soil is wet. This can result in heaving, where plants are pushed up from the soil as moisture in the soil freezes and expands. A drier, better-drained soil is kinder to plants in winter.

RIGHT PLANT, RIGHT PLACE

"Don't fight the site," so the old adage says, and those who do are usually in for more work and heartache. If you've grown plants for very long, odds are you've tried to grow a plant in a spot where, deep down, you knew it probably wouldn't be happy. Whether it's lilacs in shade, hydrangeas in dry, sun-blasted soil, or succulents on a soggy site, we've all attempted something ill-advised for the sake of ornament.

The theory of "right plant, right place" assumes that, for whatever your site throws at you, there is a beautiful plant for that spot. Yes, you can do basic and beneficial things to alter a site, like remove a sickly shrub that's shading everything around it, or add organic matter to poor soil so it retains moisture better and is richer in nutrients. If, however, you find yourself in an uphill battle to keep a plant alive with an unwieldy volume of inputs—lots of watering, lots of fertilizer, lots of maintenance—you should consider that there's likely another plant that will thrive in that place, without all the hassle. This "right plant" will be happier, which means you'll be happier. It's a win-win situation.

SOIL

Bottom Line for Plants That Thrive

Call it dirt, call it the ground, call it whatever—soil is probably the most important piece of the puzzle that is your landscape, yet it remains enigmatic to many a seasoned gardener. Plants need sunlight and water, yes, but beyond that, the soil into which they sink their roots defines them, and through that, defines the very landscape itself. In this chapter, we'll touch on the basics of soil, but if you read no further, know this: nurturing your soil is, hands down, the best way to nurture your garden.

SOIL MAKEUP AND TEXTURE

If you're anything like me, you spent half your life making footprints on top of soil, digging in it, tapping it off your boots, and washing it from under your fingernails before you considered what it's actually made of. Average soil consists of roughly 45 percent rock and mineral particles—some microscopic, some visible to the naked eye—25 percent air, 25 percent water, and 5 percent organic matter. This can vary to many degrees. Soil particles come in three types based on size. From biggest to smallest, they are sand, silt, and clay, and each has its own personality. These particles determine a soil's texture, which in turn says a lot about soil structure, and what will grow best in it. Most soils are some mix of all three, called loam.

Plants grow in all kinds of soil, from rocky to woodland.

Sand is the largest type of soil particle, and individual grains of sand can be seen with the naked eye. Because sand particles are so big, the other components of soil—air, water, and organic matter—tend to slide right through it. This can make sandy soil without amendments a challenge for growing plants, but sand also makes soil more well-drained, which is a plus.

Silt is in between sand and clay, but silt particles are exponentially smaller. Silty soil does a much better job of retaining air, water, and organic matter.

Clay is the smallest type of soil particle, and it's exponentially smaller than silt. In fact, clay particles are so tiny that they stick together and make it difficult for air, water, or organic matter to break through, or break free. Clay soil drains poorly when it gets wet, but that said, a bit of clay in soil keeps it together, whereas sandy soil falls apart.

Loam is some combination of all three. Your soil is probably loam, with either sand, silt, or clay as the major player. Loam is the ideal garden soil, because it pulls together the good characteristics of all three particle types.

There are a few methods to figure out which particle is most prevalent in your soil. To start, rub some soil between your fingers. Does it feel really gritty? Sand is likely a major component. If it's silky, your soil is probably silty. Clay-dominant soil will feel sticky. Next, take a damp handful of your soil, and make a ball with it in the palm of your hand. When you open your hand, does the ball break apart? Your soil is probably sandy. Does it stick together, but it's malleable and easily shaped? This is the sign of silty or sandy loam. If the ball sticks together well, but it's hard to break apart, there's definitely clay in your soil. The degree to which you feel each type of soil particle in these tests is a clue to your soil's overall texture. Again, most soils are loams that are some combination of each.

Did you know the soil under your feet is like a massive, interconnected series of tiny houses, each with rooms and hallways? It's true. This structure is carved out by the three other components of soil—air, water, and organic matter—as well as larger inorganic bits, like rocks, and a menagerie of living things that inhabit the soil. You're probably familiar with the air and water. Organic matter is the stuff in soil that comes from the bodies of plants and animals, like old leaves, earthworm castings, cow manure, a dead tree. The percentage of these components in soil varies based on the site.

SOIL FOOD WEB

You're probably also familiar with the fact that plants need nutrients and water from the soil to survive. How do plants access those nutrients and water? By cooperating with billions of tiny creatures in the soil.

Let's back up a minute. You've likely learned about the concept of the food chain, in which one organism dines on another and so on, and nutrients are passed upward from the first creature to the last, who finally returns those nutrients to nature when it dies. It's actually more accurate to think of the food chain as a series of connected chains, like a spider web. These are called food webs, and the soil food web is one that's particularly relevant for us.

Those tiny creatures work with plants to do all kinds of important things. Some create soil structure that allows water to trickle down into the ground; some live on plants' roots in symbiotic relationships that allow plants to access nutrients. Most of all, these tiny things are the bedrock of the soil food web, passing nutrients up to plants and then to the rest of the food web. In that sense, the life you don't see in your garden is responsible for the life you do. That's why feeding your soil is the best way to feed your garden.

SOIL TESTING

If you really want to get to know your landscape, you should test your soil. A soil test will reveal all kinds of interesting and important tidbits about your soil's makeup that are clues to what plants will thrive in it:

A soil's **pH** is the measure of its acidity or alkalinity. A pH of 7 is neutral, higher is alkaline, and lower is acidic. Soil in the Northeast tends to be acidic, but pH varies throughout the region, so it's best to test. Why? Soil pH determines how readily available nutrients are to plants. The majority of ornamental plants get the most nutrients in neutral to slightly acidic soil. If your soil is very acidic or alkaline, there are beautiful plants for you, too, but it's best to seek them out. Rhododendrons adore acidic soil, for example, while lilacs thrive in alkaline. Short-term measures can be taken to change soil pH, but it's an uphill battle, because pH is determined mostly by the soil's mineral component, which is its largest. You can buffer it a bit toward neutral by adding organic matter to your soil.

Phosphorus, potassium, calcium, and magnesium are nutrients used by plants in all kinds of ways, from aiding in photosynthesis to building plant tissue. A test will tell you if your soil is deficient in any of these elements, and offer recommendations to build them. With that in mind, it's also important to note your soil's cation exchange capacity.

Cation exchange capacity (CEC) is a long term for describing your soil's ability to exchange nutrients with plants. There's no right or wrong answer when it comes to CEC, but it's a valuable measure of how your plants jibe with your soil. CECs much lower than 10 indicate soils that have low holding capacity for nutrients, and thus a low capacity for exchanging nutrients with plants. These are usually sandy soils where nutrients naturally wash through without sticking around. Those above 10 are typically clay soils, which store many nutrients, but may make them difficult for plants to access. Again, adding organic matter to soil generally adds more plant-accessible nutrients to lean soils, and helps make locked-up nutrients in heavy soils more available, but it's generally best to also search for plants that thrive in either situation.

Organic matter is, as we've discussed, the soil component that comes from plants and animals. A soil test will tell you the percentage of organic matter in your soil.

Soil testing is typically inexpensive, and involves sending a bit of your soil to your local agricultural extension or a soil lab. Soil testing resources can be found at the back of this book. The moral of the soil-testing story is this: nurturing your soil will nurture your garden, and testing your soil will illustrate how your soil may need to be nurtured.

The lowly worm is one of many beneficial creatures that inhabit your garden.

GARDEN DWELLERS

Landscape Cohabitants to Love and Loathe

Since the landscape is an ecosystem, like it or not, you'll be sharing it with other creatures—yes, creatures that may prove a detriment to the garden, but just as many or more that will find it the same wonderland you do, and reward you for making them at home. The degree of different kinds of life in an ecosystem is called biodiversity. The more biodiversity you encourage in your garden, the more likely those beneficial creatures will be there to keep pests in check. That's how nature operates when ecosystems are left undisturbed.

While we can only scratch the surface in discussing these critters here, it's important to at least touch on them, so you have a sense of who's who in the veritable zoo that lies just outside your backdoor.

BENEFICIALS

Beneficial creatures play a role in just about every good thing that happens in your garden. Are your plants growing well? That's due in part to soil organisms that help them collect nutrients from the ground, as well as those that dig around and make for good soil structure. Above ground, larger animals pollinate plants and pick off more pesky critters. All contribute to the soil food web. But let's not get ahead of ourselves. Here's a quick survey of beneficial life you're likely to find in a healthy landscape.

Soil Organisms

Billions of tiny creatures inhabit your soil, and as we've discussed, these critters are a big part of what makes soil work for plants.

Bacteria and fungi do all kinds of important things. They break down decomposing organic matter, extracting its nutrients. Many live in symbiotic relationships with plants, on or around their roots, which exude chemicals to feed them, and are in turn protected from disease by the bacteria and fungi. Mycorrhizal fungi are particularly known for this, as well as their ability to aid roots' nutrient intake.

Tiny animals like protozoa, nematodes, and micro-arthropods like mites, as well as earthworms and beetles feed on bacteria and fungi, and in turn release nutrients they've stored into the soil for plants to use. They also build soil structure that's so important for plants—those tiny rooms and hallways we talked about earlier.

Insects

All insects are creepy-crawly and bad, right? Not at all—in fact, many are your first line of defense against bugs that are bad. We call these garden do-gooders beneficial insects. The reason they're beneficial is pretty simple: lots of them eat those bad bugs. Lots of others pollinate plants, a process essential for plants to set seed.

Butterflies pollinate flowers—and they're beautiful.

Among the predators is everyone's favorite insect, the ladybug. It's more accurately referred to as the lady beetle, and it feeds on small, sucking insects like aphids. Not every wasp is prone to stinging humans—many tiny wasps scour the landscape for eggs and larvae of other insects, including those that will feast on your plants. Lacewings' larvae eat all kinds of bad bugs, while ground beetles attack grubs and other pests under the soil. Dragonflies do double duty: besides being beautiful, they prey on adult and larval mosquitoes. While technically arachnids, spiders play an important role in catching flying insects as well.

Of course, the most sought-after garden insects are the pollinators. Even if you're not a fan of those creepy-crawlies, it's tough not to appreciate the beauty of a butterfly sipping nectar from a plant in your garden on a summer afternoon. Many gardeners welcome bees as well, and beekeeping at home is enjoying a resurgence in popularity. Even if your plants don't need to reseed, encouraging your native pollinator population supports your larger native ecosystem as well. Those little guys also pollinate wild plants that need them to survive, and they play a vital role in the food web your entire ecosystem is based on as well.

Birds

Few animals are more sought after as landscape visitors than birds. The winged creatures have delighted humans for centuries, for both their beauty and music.

If you've ever watched birds hunt and peck through your yard, you know a healthy bird population also feasts on all kinds of insects. No stone is left unturned. Robins poke through the lawn, while chickadees patrol the trunks of trees. The biggest and littlest of the avian clan have special jobs all their own. While hummingbirds pollinate plants, hawks and other large raptors prey on rodent pests like rabbits and voles.

A Baltimore oriole enjoying a crabapple tree.

Save the Bees!

The humble, hardworking honeybee isn't just responsible for making the honey you eat. This little gal and her sisters (all worker bees are female) live for the hefty task of pollinating fruit and vegetable crops grown for food—crops that don't necessarily produce food if they aren't pollinated. Over the past several years, honeybee colonies have collapsed in an alarming trend across North America and Europe.

Scientists puzzled over the source of honeybee die-off, a phenomenon named colony collapse disorder, for several years, at various points looking to pests and diseases bees are prone to. In 2013, new research from a number of sources found that three pesticides (clothianidin, imidacloprid, and thiamethoxam) in a class called neonicotinoids were to blame. Unfortunately, these are the most widely used agricultural pesticides today.

While the debate as to how to prevent more bee die-off continues, what can you do to keep your bees? For starters, if you choose to use a pesticide, choose one that doesn't contain these chemicals. Plant non-treated plants for your local bee population, and if you're shopping, inquire at your nursery as to whether they're aware if the plants they sell have been treated—indeed, it was discovered in 2013 that many plants marketed as bee-friendly had been treated with neonicotinoid pesticides. If a nursery grows its own plants, they will be able to tell you. If you really want to help save the bees, look up your local beekeeping society. These organizations have enjoyed renewed popularity, even in urban areas, and usually offer courses in beekeeping for any kind of garden.

To make your landscape more hospitable to birds, pay attention to what they look for most: food, water, and shelter. Provide more food for birds by populating your garden with plants they love, and making your garden more hospitable to insects. That formal garden may be pretty, but biodiversity is higher in wilder, more unkempt landscapes. That means more insects for birds to hunt. Wilder landscapes also mean more bird shelter, and birds are a wily, wary bunch, so any extra protection is welcome to them. Evergreens and thick deciduous shrubs are favorites, and thorny plants protect better from predators. Finally, as anyone with a birdbath knows, birds adore water, and a little goes a long way.

Other Animals

Birds may be the first beneficial animal that pops into your head, but they're a single group among many you'd do well to invite into your garden. While these creatures may not be as sexy, theirs are crucial roles to play. Bats, frogs, snakes, and fish are predators that see your garden as an all-you-can-eat buffet of insects and other creatures, like slugs, many of which can be harmful in the landscape. A single bat can consume half its body weight in insects in one summer night. Make these creatures at home in your garden by providing them with a water source, like a low birdbath or pond; giving them shelter in the form of a full garden, not a plane of mulch polka-dotted by plants; and exercising caution with pesticides and herbicides that can cause them harm. They'll return the favor by snacking on creatures you'd prefer didn't get comfy.

PESTS

Like it or not, every landscape comes with a merry band of scalawags we call pests, and you will encounter them in some form, at some point. Best to educate yourself a bit about each one so you know what you're up against, and where to start when it comes to getting rid of them, or living with them.

One popular approach to managing pests in the landscape is integrated pest management (IPM). IPM relies on common-sense methods and a multifaceted approach to pest control. You can make an IPM plan for your yard. It's as simple as four steps, in this order:

1. Draw the line. Every garden has pests, and like it or not, pests have their place in your garden. It's important to know your threshold. When you discover evidence of pests, ask yourself at what point will they have crossed the line? A hole or two in your lilies' leaves isn't cause to spray them with a pesticide. The discovery of lily leaf beetle, however, requires quick action, as well as step 2.

2. Keep an eye out. Educate yourself about these varmints, all the better to keep tabs on them, or telltale signs of them, in your garden. We'll touch on how to deal with a few pests here, but the Recommended Reading appendix includes a list of references on pests and diseases. You can decide where the line is for each. A solitary chipmunk burrow may be no big deal until it's taken over by rats. Best to watch it.

3. Stay ahead of them. Common-sense methods of prevention go a very long way in pest control, and can save you a lot of work and heartache. Learn what to do to make your garden less hospitable to those pests, and you may not have to deal with them at all. Deer, for example, may make their way through your yard on a nightly basis, but if you populate your garden with plants they don't like to eat, they'll move on to the neighbors' hostas.

Why Grow Plant Invaders When You Can Grow Sustainable All-Stars?

You may be wondering why a few popular plants listed here don't make other appearances in this book. Bad news: it's because these plants have been recognized as invasive species in the Northeast. The good news is that plenty of beautiful alternatives do the same things and then some. Here's a survey of northeastern plant invaders and all-star alternatives:

Burning bush (*Euonymus alatus*) is an invasive species in the Northeast.

INVADER	ALTERNATIVE
Asian bittersweet (*Celastrus orbiculatus*)	Chinese trumpet creeper (*Campsis grandiflora* 'Morning Calm')
Red-leaved barberry (*Berberis thunbergii* cultivars, *B. vulgaris* cultivars)	'Little Devil' ninebark (*Physocarpus opulifolius* 'Little Devil')
Variegated bishop's weed (*Aegopodium podagraria* 'Variegatum')	Carpet bugle (*Ajuga reptans* cultivars)
Burning bush (*Euonymus alatus*)	Itea (*Itea virginica* cultivars)
Common and border privet (*Ligustrum obtusifolium, L. vulgare*)	Inkberry (*Ilex glabra* cultivars)
Japanese honeysuckle (*Lonicera japonica*)	'Major Wheeler' honeysuckle (*Lonicera sempervirens* 'Major Wheeler')
Norway maple (*Acer platanoides*)	Red maple (*Acer rubrum*)
Reed canary grass (*Phalaris arundinacea*)	Variegated feather reed grass (*Calamagrostis acutiflora* 'Overdam')
Shrub honeysuckle (*Lonicera ×bella, L. maackii, L. morrowii, L. tatarica*)	Mock orange (*Philadelphus coronarius*)
Yellow flag iris (*Iris pseudacorus*)	Blue flag iris (*Iris versicolor*)

4. Control them. So you've drawn the line, identified a pest that's moved in even though you worked proactively to prevent it—now it's time to take action. Start with the method of control that's most effective while making the fewest waves among the rest of your garden, and work up to the big guns if you have to. After all, woody invasive species won't return if you yank them the right way. No need to douse them in herbicide first, which risks spraying other plants and harming beneficial insect and soil life.

Weeds

Even the novice gardener is familiar with the concept of weeds, but how well do you really know weeds? Like it or not, weeds are Mother Nature's most tenacious troops, sent to the front line over and over to colonize the sidewalk cracks and abandoned lots where your impatiens would never dream of growing. As noble as that may be, weeds are completely undiscerning, and they'll gleefully colonize your flowerbed too. That's when they become a problem.

The novice gardener also knows the most effective way to combat weeds is to pull them, especially before they set seed. This is true in almost every case, and weeding is the most common maintenance task you'll likely face. Here are some other tips to combat weeds:

- **Mulch.** A generous layer of mulch keeps weeds at bay. Nature sees the ground is covered; no need

Weeds need little introduction.

to cover it with weeds. If the area you're mulching is especially weedy, a couple of layers of black-and-white newspaper followed by mulch smothers weeds even more effectively.
- **Plant.** A full garden smothers many a weed seedling. Groundcovers work especially well.
- **Tread lightly.** Disturbing the soil tickles weed seeds that hang out in the ground for years, waiting for just that opportunity. That's one reason why weeds inevitably grow up in your flowerbed, where you've disturbed the soil to plant plants. If you need to walk through your beds, consider stepping stones.

Beyond the "garden variety" weeds you'll find in your landscape lurks a more insidious gang of plant pests. These are invasive species: non-native plants that make their way into our native ecosystems, and find conditions so fabulous and free of natural predators that they crowd out native plants. Don't be confused by the name—while you may have heard weeds and garden plants that tend to spread referred to as "invasive," true invasive species are an ecological breed apart. While weeds are tenacious in gardens, invasive species can be steamrollers, nearly impossible to eradicate. Likewise, most weeds can be controlled by pulling or smothering, but many invasive species only respond to chemical pesticides like glyphosate, and often require repeated applications of that. If you'd like to ID your weeds and invasive species, check the Recommended Reading appendix for Northeast weed references.

Insects

Insect pests are the subject of a library all their own. I've listed a few references for pests in Recommended Reading. Because it can be tough to tell the difference between beneficial insects and pesky ones, identification and prevention are your best friends when it comes to fighting insect pests. The big, fat caterpillar you're alarmed to see chewing on your milkweed is very likely the larvae of everyone's favorite flying bug, the monarch butterfly. Beneficials may make a few holes in your plants here and there, but their overall impact in the landscape is a positive. Bad bugs, on the other hand, do more harm than good. Learn what they like and how to identify their calling cards, and you'll be better equipped to fight them.

Japanese beetle is a common insect pest.

Slugs aren't insects, but shell-less mollusks, and their love of dining on leafy greens under the cover of dark can be a particular headache for gardeners. Fortunately, all kinds of small animals and birds eat slugs, so if you make these predators at home in your garden, you won't fight the slugs alone. One age-old method of combatting slugs is to place a

Insect Invaders

Though any insect pests can be a problem, insects that are invasive species pose an even greater challenge, as these critters have found their way into our ecosystems (where they have no natural predators) from their homelands (where they do). Here's a sampling of invasive bugs to learn and know:

Asian longhorned beetle (*Anoplophora glabripennis*). This large, black beetle has white spots and long antennae. Its larvae bore holes into the heart of deciduous trees. Once this happens, it's too late for the tree, but reporting is critical to prevent the beetle's spread. As of this writing, the beetle has been found in New York and Massachusetts, as well as neighboring Ohio. Look out for shallow scars in tree bark, sawdust near the base of trees, dead branches, dime-sized holes—or the beetle itself. Treatment is strictly professional.

Emerald ash borer (*Agrilus planipennis*). Larvae of this tiny, brilliantly green beetle feed on the inner bark of ash trees (*Fraxinus* species), damaging the tree and even killing it. It's been discovered in states and provinces from Quebec and Ontario to North Carolina, and west as far as Kansas. This little beetle has a similar native counterpart, but it's bigger and its body more elongated, while the emerald ash borer is smaller and fatter. When it opens its wings to fly, you'll see its abdomen is a shiny red color. Signs of emerald ash borer infestation include die-off of a portion of an ash's crown, a new cluster of shoots at the base of a tree, and evidence of serpentine trails left by larvae if the bark is removed. Again, treatment is strictly professional.

Japanese beetle (*Popillia japonica*). A common and unmistakable landscape pest, this round, shiny beetle is the bane of rose fans everywhere, but it has a taste for all kinds of plants. Beetle grubs feed on lawn too, and can be controlled with a bacterial inoculant called milky spore. The adults can be picked off or shaken into jars and killed fairly easily. Neem oil also works well, as does coupling beetle-prone plants with poisonous plants the beetles also love, like four o'clocks (*Mirabilis* cultivars) and castor bean (*Ricinus communis* cultivars).

Lily leaf beetle (*Lilioceris lilii*). Native to Europe but discovered in Montreal in the 1940s, this disgusting little bug didn't travel any farther until the 1990s, and it's now a common sight in the northern parts of the Northeast. Why is it disgusting? Because adult beetles protect their larvae by coating them with their own feces, and dozens will decimate your lilies in a flash. Fortunately, both the bright orange adults and their odious offspring are pretty easy to catch and squash—just keep a very watchful eye on those lilies, and you may escape with only a hole or two. Spraying with neem oil works well, too.

Viburnum leaf beetle (*Pyrrhalta viburni*). This beetle has a taste for viburnum, as its name suggests, and has been making its way across the Northeast. Their nesting sites appear as rows of tiny brown bumps on viburnum, and you can spot prune them out and burn them in winter, when the shrubs are leafless. Otherwise, try to keep an eye out for larvae (yellow-brown caterpillars with black spots, likely no more than a half-inch long), or the tiny brown adults. Methods of prevention include encouraging beneficial insects that feed on beetle larvae, and planting resistant species of viburnum, including Korean spice viburnum (*Viburnum carlesii*) and snowball viburnum (*V. plicatum* var. *tomentosum*).

Winter moth (*Operophtera brumata*). Across the Northeast, after temperatures cool in fall and during nights all through winter, millions of winter moths emerge from the soil to lay eggs on the bark of trees. Their nearly invisible larvae hatch in spring and waste no time chowing down on those trees' emerging leaves. If your late-spring trees suddenly look like Swiss cheese, winter moth is most likely to blame. Professional treatment is your best bet, but it has to be done before the damage is done. If your trees are already looking chewed, make a note for next year. The pros trust a spray called spinosad. Made from a soil bacterium, it is organic and incredibly effective, but should be used on cloudy days before or after a tree has bloomed—otherwise it can kill honeybees.

Hemlock woolly adelgid (*Adelges tsugae*). Last and tiniest but certainly not least, this itty bitty pest has infected native stands and garden specimens of hemlock (*Tsuga canadensis*) across North America. The bugs themselves are nearly imperceptible, but look for the "wool" they create near the young tips of branches of hemlock in spring. These are egg masses, and would be a bit smaller than the tip of a cotton swab. The adelgid is a sucking insect that feeds on the trees' sap, and because they're so small and can damage a tree quickly, professional treatment is best. Moreover, hemlock prefers deep, damp soil, and young trees appreciate shade. This little pest is especially attracted to weak trees that are poorly sited in hot, dry sites.

dish of cheap beer on the ground in your garden at night. Slugs are attracted to it, crawl in, and drown.

Mosquitoes make for incredibly inhospitable conditions for humans in gardens, and spread diseases like West Nile virus and eastern equine encephalitis (EEE). Take care to eliminate sources of standing water in the garden, and you'll decrease these tiny biters' breeding ground. Encouraging mosquito predators, like birds and dragonflies, helps to a small degree, but you can use all the help you can get! Many methods of mosquito protection are available, to varying degrees of effectiveness. The surefire mosquito repellent typically contains DEET, but many gardeners swear by botanical sprays. Try them and decide what's best for you.

Plant Diseases

As with insect pests, plant diseases could fill up a room with books of their own. Diseases, often called pathogens, come in three forms you should know: bacteria, fungi, and viruses. That's right—as with insects, there are good and bad apples in this bunch of organisms. Many bacteria are beneficial, but some cause disease. Bacterial diseases can be tough to treat, because bacteria are tiny, and spread more quickly and easily. Unlike beneficial fungi, the fungi to watch out for are the parasitic kind—those that suck your plants' energy, rather than supply it.

Prevention works incredibly well in fighting plant diseases. All of these pathogens can be transmitted both by means beyond your control—wind, rain, insects—but also by you. Keep your tools and hands clean. If you follow the "right plant, right place" method of gardening to grow healthy plants, you're already on the right track. In a nutshell, assess your site's conditions, choose plants that will thrive in them, and you'll have a healthy and largely disease-free garden. Choose a plant that will struggle in your garden because it's too wet or dry, sunny or shady, and that plant will become a magnet for diseases, which could, in turn, infect others. If you suspect a plant has a disease, the first step to learning how to treat it is to identify it—remember, knowledge is power. See Recommended Reading for a list of references for further reading on disease ID, treatment, and prevention.

Deer

Deer are by far the most common large animal that may pay your garden a visit, as well as the most destructive. Before the twentieth century, much of the Northeast's old-growth forest was logged and given over to farmland, and deer populations dropped precipitously. In the mid-1800s in New England alone, it's estimated only 30 to 40 percent of land was left as forest. Fortunately, that number (born out over the entire region) has rebounded to around 80 percent today. White-tailed deer (*Odocoileus virginianus*) have made a comeback along with the trees—a more dubious resurgence for we gardeners. Because they've grown up with us, today's deer are more comfortable living among humans. In our densely populated region, that means they're more likely to make a buffet out of your landscape.

While I've labeled deer-resistant plants earlier in this book, it's important to note that hungry deer will eat just about anything—hence the term "deer-resistant," as opposed to "deerproof." What exactly deer decide to snack on in your garden greatly depends on your plants' inherent palatability (hostas are a favorite), how accessible your garden is to deer, the amount of other nearby vegetation they may decide to munch on first, and the number of hungry mouths in your local herd. (The bigger the herd, the bigger and more indiscriminate their appetite.) You may have heard and read about various methods to keep deer at bay, but in the end, two methods work best: gardening with deer-resistant plants, and having a professional install a deer fence.

For fencing, either double up or go tall. A 7- to 8-ft. fence from the ground up typically does the trick. Another trick that works well is a pair of shorter fences, 5 ft. or less, spaced around 5 ft. apart and parallel to each, as deer tend to be a bit claustrophobic and would rather browse outside than jump into and through that narrow space between the two fences to get at your garden.

In the Northeast, keeping deer out isn't just good for your garden, it's good for your health. Deer carry the deer tick (*Ixodes scapularis*), notorious as the bearer of Lyme disease. The tick transfers Lyme to larger animals, like deer, pets, and people, from rodents. Scientists have debated whether or not controlling deer populations effectively reduces the disease, but feeding on large animals is key to the deer tick's reproductive cycle, after which females drop to the ground to lay eggs. A two-pronged approach of controlling your garden's rodent population (which is a good idea anyway) while keeping deer out is likely your safest bet.

Rodents

Aside from deer, the biological order Rodentia will likely do the most damage in your landscape. Mice and voles see your garden as their meal ticket, and since they're small, their nibbling at the base of plants often goes unnoticed until it's too late. Rabbits are bigger and more brazen. On top of that, both are prone to damaging small trees in winter, when food is scarce, by chewing a ring around the base—a problem called girdling. Chipmunks and squirrels prove less problematic, although the former digs burrows that can disturb plants' roots, and both have a taste for bulbs. Rats are common pests in cities, suburbs, and the country, and though typically drawn to veggies, they'll eat any plant they decide is tasty, and they carry diseases to boot.

Groundhogs are just that, and will devour plants from below before you know what hit you. Many and varied members of the rodent clan carry Lyme disease. For all of these reasons, it's best to keep rodents in your garden at bay, and that's best done with a little ingenuity, a lot of common sense, and even more patience.

Consider your threshold. A vole here and there is probably nothing to worry about, but learn to identify signs of voles and other rodents, and make your garden less attractive to rodents. Search for plants that are beautiful but less palatable, and mix these in with others. Daffodil bulbs, for example, can effectively deter squirrels from eating tulip bulbs because they taste bad. Mulch is vital to nourishing plants' roots, but if you suspect voles live in your neighborhood, mulch with straight compost. A coarser mulch like leaf mold can make the perfect veil under which critters will invade. Keep brush piles and other likely potential boarding places (a stack of old bricks, for example) as separate as possible from the parts of your garden you'd like to keep rodent-free. Ornamental grasses can be beautiful left unpruned in winter, but they make perfect nesting sites when matted down by snow, so cut them down if you sense trouble.

Control methods for rodents vary from animal to animal. Trapping works well for many, especially with concealed traps they can access without straying into the open. Smoke bombs can be an effective method to eradicate burrowing rodents, but it's important to find and block all their points of egress. See Recommended Reading for more information on pest control.

Chipmunks are adorable, but they can be a nuisance in the garden.

Key Duties of Plant Care

You've designed a garden, assessed your site, and now you're ready to plant. How to make that garden grow? In this section, we'll talk about the growing needs of plants, and all the little things you'll need to do to help your landscape flourish and be as fruitful as possible.

COMPOSTING

Many new gardeners are mystified by compost, but composting is, in fact, one of the simplest ways both to produce good stuff to make your garden grow and to cut down on the waste you put at the curb. If you've got space, why not compost? Remember, compost feeds the soil, and if you feed your soil, your soil will, in turn, feed your plants.

Compost is defined as organic matter that's broken down almost completely into a soil-like substance called humus. Compost brings all the benefits of organic matter we've talked about to your soil, in a form that's already so decomposed that it incorporates into the soil more quickly.

There are many composting bins and systems on the market today, but whether you decide to bin it or pile it up in a heap, composting requires three simple steps:

Good compost is organic matter at its best.

1. Start with three parts "browns." Browns are dry items that come from plants, either directly (fall leaves) or indirectly (paper towels), and are full of carbon. They make up the larger part of your compost.

2. Add one part "greens." Greens are nitrogen-filled materials, and tend to be fresher vegetative items, like grass clippings, coffee grounds, and bits of veggies you didn't need.

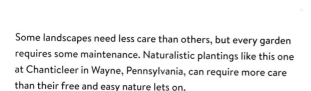

Some landscapes need less care than others, but every garden requires some maintenance. Naturalistic plantings like this one at Chanticleer in Wayne, Pennsylvania, can require more care than their free and easy nature lets on.

What You Can and Can't Compost

(G)=green, (B)=brown

Do compost:

- Fruit and veggie discards—peel, cores, rinds (G)
- Coffee grounds and filters (G)
- Paper towels and napkins (B)
- Tea bags, leaves included (G)
- Shredded, non-glossy newspaper (B)
- Grass clippings (G)
- Eggshells (G)
- Most bread and bread products—no buttery desserts (G)
- Rabbit, hamster, gerbil, or guinea pig manure—but allow a few months for it to break down well before using in the garden (G)
- Shredded, thin cardboard, including toilet paper rolls (B)
- Plain, cooked rice, pasta, or quinoa (G)
- Fall leaves (B)
- Pruning leftovers and dead houseplants, as long as they're small or well shredded if they're woody (G)
- Weeds that will not set seed or take root—be wary and ID them first to be sure (G)

Don't compost:

- Meat or other animal bits
- Dairy products
- Dog or cat manure, or that of other carnivorous pets
- Oils or other cooking media, like lard
- Peanut butter—too high in fat, though bread with a bit of peanut butter is no problem
- Weeds that will set seed or take root
- Invasive plant species

3. Mix your greens and browns all together, or layer them. Either way, throw in a shovel-full of rich soil or already-made compost, because this will get things started. Turn the mixture once a week or so to let oxygen in, and keep it from drying out. In a few months, you'll have compost to use in your garden.

If your compost starts to smell, it could be for a few reasons. The most likely scenario is too few browns and too many greens. The ratio of these two is called the carbon to nitrogen, or C:N, ratio. Adding some browns will likely solve the problem. If your compost gets an ammonia scent, that means it hasn't been stirred enough. Animal or meat products shouldn't be added to compost (see "What You Can and Can't Compost"), and will produce unpleasant odors and attract undesired wild animals.

MULCHING

When you hear the word "mulch," you probably think of chopped up bark and wood chips used to cover the ground in flowerbeds. You're not far off. The term mulch actually refers to anything used to cover ground, bark and wood chips included. In the Northeast, our climate and soil are such that, if ground is bare, Mother Nature will cover it with something—usually those most tenacious plants that are the first to colonize a naked patch of ground. We tend to call them weeds. Given that, if your ground is bare and you're not looking to grow weeds, it's essential you cover it up.

Besides blocking weeds, mulch offers a number of other benefits. It prevents topsoil erosion (keeping the nutritious stuff in the soil from washing away), and mulches that come from living things—wood, bark, compost, leaves—ultimately break down and enrich soil as well. In doing that, mulch adds organic matter to the soil, which in turn makes soil more moisture-retentive and builds soil structure.

Shredded wood and bark is the best-known mulch on the market.

Plants appreciate that, and many also appreciate the cooling effect mulch has on their roots in summer, when it acts like sunblock, and the insulation it provides in winter, like a comfy sweater. You'll find many forms of mulch on the market. While many a mulch is beneficial, there's a right way and wrong way to go about mulching.

Do

Go long. Spread a relatively thin layer of mulch over a large area, rather than a thicker mulch over a small area. Around herbaceous plants, 2–3 in. is enough, 3–4 in. for trees and shrubs, and no mulch up against the trunks of trees, or around the crowns of other plants.

Mulch with compost. Compost makes excellent mulch, especially because you can plant directly into it.

Replenish mulch every year or two, in spring. If you use a mulch that breaks down, like bark, check to see how much has broken down before you freshen it—if it's breaking down slowly, you run the risk of mulching too deeply. Mulches like gravel that don't break down will begin to work their way into the soil, especially when used for footpaths, but can be freshened annually by raking. Gravel, and other mulches that consist of small particles, will need to be topped off more often than those with big particles, like rocks and stones.

Don't

Choke a tree with mulch. A cone of mulch piled up around the base of a tree is called a "mulch volcano," and it's effectively a slow, undignified death sentence for your poor tree. Mulch volcanoes cause roots to grow out of the side of the tree, above its root collar. Having nowhere else to go, they grow

Mulch Materials

Thumbs Up!

Bark, shredded and chipped wood. Wood mulches come in many varieties, from coarse "playground mulch" to shredded hemlock, spruce, and pine. When searching for wood mulches, choose not for color or consistency, but for how well the mulch will break down—if at all. An undyed mulch that's well shredded will do all the good things we've talked about above. A coarsely chipped mulch, on the other hand, can take years to decay if your soil isn't healthy or the mulch is piled too deeply, as well as leaching valuable nutrients from soil. This is great strictly for weed blocking, but not great for soil and plants. Newly chipped wood mulch can damage herbaceous plants. Your mulch should not have to travel a great distance to get to you—ask where it comes from! The more local your mulch source (within your metro area, state, or at least within the Northeast), the better the odds you can confirm firsthand it doesn't contain dubious materials like ground-up construction debris.

Compost. Straight compost makes an excellent mulch, and you can plant right into it, too. Fine compost doesn't quite have the water-retaining qualities of bark, so if it's hot, be sure to add a bit more than you would for bark.

Cocoa and buckwheat hulls. Relative newcomers on the mulch scene, these are food industry by-products, and make fine mulches, even if they're a bit pricey. Cocoa shells in particular smell nice and darken with age, but use them carefully around dogs, as the scent may attract them, and cocoa and canines don't mix. Some brands advertise themselves as more pet-friendly, but it's always better to be safe.

Crushed seashells. If you're looking to make your landscape instantly reminiscent of the seaside, look no further than crushed shells as mulch. Often used for driveways, shell mulch doesn't add the same organic matter to soil, but it does add minerals and raise soil pH a bit, if your soil is too acidic.

Rocks and gravel. Like crushed shells, stone mulches are aesthetically appealing, even if they're not an appreciable source of nutrients for plants. A stone mulch does, however, last forever, as long as it's kept clear of organic matter like leaves that would bury it.

Living mulch. What about mulch that's alive? Groundcovers do all the good things bark mulch does, and can be a lot more interesting.

Thumbs Down

Dyed wood. Many mulches are dyed to be a specific color. Not only do those dyes not last the season, they trickle down into the soil. There's a lot of debate as to whether mulch dyes are harmful to soil, but why take the risk? More than that, the wood that these mulches come from typically has a checkered past as shipping palettes or other industrial materials. It can contain all kinds of odd substances from its former life.

Rubber. Rubber mulch comes from ground-up tires, which contain all kinds of toxic chemicals that aren't good for soil life, or the people digging in it.

Landscape fabric. Weed-blocking landscape fabrics can be effective if used under stone mulches. Otherwise, if you layer fabric under any mulch material that breaks down over time, the fabric's pores will become clogged, air and water won't effectively reach your soil, and soil life will head for the hills as soil structure breaks down. Weeds, ironically, always find a way to break through landscape fabric, and they will be the first to colonize your damaged soil when you remove it.

around the tree in a circle, ultimately strangling it. Mulch volcanoes also look ridiculous.

Rob your soil of nutrients by mulching too deeply. If you layer bark mulch more than 3–4 in., it actually leaches valuable nutrients out of the soil, away from plants, and its breakdown slows significantly.

Waste time, money, and energy on too much mulch. If you realize the surface of your mature flowerbed is mostly bark mulch, as opposed to plants, you're probably expending resources replenishing an excessive amount of mulch that breaks down each year. Plants also grow naturally in communities, not in solitude in a sea of mulch. No, you don't need to grow a jungle, and yes, it's okay for your plants to look like polka dots while they're growing in, but if you prefer simplicity, consider a gravel garden, or groundcovers. Your wallet and your back will thank you.

WATERING

Water is one of the building blocks of life, and plants are no exception. Every plant will need water, whether it comes from your garden hose, or naturally from the sky. In the Northeast, we're generally blessed with an abundance of water, unlike other regions of North America. Even so, our region is no stranger to drought, and water can become scarce here, especially when winter snowmelt and seasonal rainfall are less than usual. Dry spells aren't uncommon in summer, and while downpours do help, citizens in towns with watering bans are often puzzled when they don't fix the problem—that's because periodic downpours may not be enough to replenish reservoirs for drinking water, above or below ground. It takes steady, sustained showers to really soak the ground.

All plants will need to be watered for at least a portion of their first growing season to get their roots established—once a day at first, then tapering off to once every few days, and once a week. The best time of day to water is either early morning or in the evening. (Watering midday means your plants will lose much of that moisture to evaporation.) All plants benefit from the deeper, prolonged watering that promotes better root growth than a quick spray from the hose. Drip tube irrigation works perfectly, but a soaker hose buried under mulch, while not quite as effective, is the quickest, easiest solution for most home gardeners. Trees and shrubs transplanted from large pots or balled and burlapped will need more time to settle in—probably one whole growing season—and are best watered with drip bags or tubes that can be filled with water periodically, and watered deeply over a period of many hours. Plant in spring or fall, when rains are plentiful, and you can rely more heavily on Mother Nature to water your new babies. If you've assessed your site well, populated it with plants that suit your soil, and mulched well, the vast majority of plants should never need more water than what falls from the sky in our region, once they're established.

PRUNING

Don't be afraid of pruning—but be wary of overdoing it! It would seem the vast majority of gardeners are either overcautious or overzealous when it comes to pruning. The former let their shrubs grow off the charts for fear of doing them harm. The latter diligently prune their shrubs into bubbles and boxes, with little regard to those shrubs' natural form.

Fear not, intrepid pruners, there is a middle ground, and it's simple. First, start with plants that will grow to an appropriate size and shape. Second, prune those plants to maintain that size and shape. That can mean an annual trim (hedging plants), an annual chop to the ground (cut-back shrubs like butterfly bush, catalpa, and beautyberry), or, for the vast majority of others, a simple snip here and there to keep them shapely or in bounds. That's it!

Pruning should also be viewed as a practice that not only keeps plants in line, but stimulates them to grow more, and where you'd prefer they grow. Look closely at your shrub, and you'll find each stem is made up of many sections. Find a node along that stem, where a few offshoots grow outward from it. If you snip off growth above those offshoots, they'll be stimulated to grow in its place. Thus, if you give your evergreens a flattop, they'll give you new growth at their tops, and get leggy at the base. Better to shear them a bit closer at the top and leave them wider at the base—this allows light to reach their legs, and means you'll be rewarded with fuller plants, not inverted pyramids.

On a more practical level, pruning can be the answer to rejuvenating overgrown, unkempt plants, as well as those that may have fallen victim to pests and diseases.

Here are a few basic pruning concepts:

Shearing is a common practice for dense hedging plants, and is often used less effectively for others. To shear a plant is to cut a plane clean across it, as with electric hedge trimmers. You may also trim more judiciously with manual pruners, if you're bothered by the idea of cutting haphazardly through leaves, but most hedging plants will bounce back from shearing just fine. If you find yourself prone to shearing large-leaved plants, think twice. This is a sign you should consider replacing that rhodie with something like boxwood or yew.

Restoration is when a plant is cut severely to stimulate new, better growth. It's a practice that can work phenomenally well to rejuvenate the overgrown and neglected trees and shrubs that greet many new homeowners. Effective restoration pruning varies from plant to plant, so do some research to find out how best to restore your shrub before you cut.

Deadheading, a completely different kind of pruning, is the practice of removing spent blooms from flowering plants. Deadheading is often done to make a garden look neater, though plants with flowers that remain interesting even after they've gone past have become increasingly popular. Deadheading may also prompt a new flush of growth in plants that bloom over a long period.

Timing for pruning varies, but there are a few good rules of thumb. Flowering plants are best pruned soon after their flowers fade. Often, shrubs will put out new growth one year and bloom from that growth the next. (Hydrangeas are the classic example of this.) Given that, it's best to deadhead and do any pruning for size just after flowers fade, so the plant will have time left in the growing season to send out new shoots for next year's flowers.

Foliage plants, including those that are sheared, are best pruned to shape in late winter, before new growth emerges in spring, but can benefit from a trim anytime. Large trees, on the other hand, are some of the biggest foliage plants of all, and come with their own special standards for pruning. This is usually best done with the expertise and help of an arborist.

Deadwood can and should be pruned out at any time of year, as its removal will stimulate fresh growth. Likewise, isolating some types of disease- and pest-infested growth is best too, although timing varies—start by identifying the pest or disease, and then you can discover whether pruning is the answer.

There are many styles of pruning, but all should be beneficial to plants.

CLEANUP

For better or worse, many plants tend to make messes, and as the steward of your garden, it's your job to clean them up. In choosing plants, consider this closely. That maple may be beautiful, but when it grows up, you'll have leaves to rake. A tree with tiny leaves may mean less cleanup.

Fall in particular is the time of year we consider cleanup most. When it comes to those fall leaves, you have a few choices besides raking and getting rid of them. Leaves can make an excellent mulch if left to break down in beds, assuming there's no vole population, but even then, a thin layer of shredded leaves does a garden good. Bigger leaves like oak

Cleanup comes part and parcel with gardening.

leaves may mat down and should be cleared away, and leaves shouldn't be left on lawns over winter, as that can invite diseases. Of course, leaves can be composted, if your compost heap is big enough.

Many cities and towns throughout the Northeast have composting sites, where you can drop off leaves and brush. Others do curbside pickup of yard waste. Burning can be an effective way to clean up too, but be sure to check local regulations on when you can burn and where—wildfires present real danger in dry periods. It should go without saying that weeds should be disposed of separately from compost, as they may populate it with seeds, and special care should be taken to completely dispose of invasive species, most of which would be thrilled to come back from the dead and infest your compost heap. Your town's composting site may also offer compost for your garden—be wary of it, for these reasons. If the town's heap is professionally cooked and maintained, it may be terrific. If not, it may be a backdoor for weeds into your landscape.

Finally, if you clean your tools, they'll hold up longer. Remove caked-on dirt and debris, and for pruning tools, a periodic dip with a household cleaner like Lysol helps prevent the spread of diseases.

LETTING GO

Like it or not, if you grow plants, you will kill plants. Don't take it personally. The most seasoned gardeners leave a trail of destruction in their wake, over the course of many years. Despite our best efforts, plants die.

That said, sometimes our propensity for nurturing plants gets the better of us, and we find ourselves hobbling a plant that's too far gone. Yes, plants are resilient, and it's possible to bring a near-dead plant back to life, but it often involves a lot of work and even more heartache. More than that, plants in distress often attract pests and diseases that are eager to pick off a weak member of the herd, and spread to neighbors if they can.

Looking for one more great reason to compost? Give your plant a second life in the compost heap, and remember, removing a plant that's sad and struggling means you've got the chance to choose something exciting and new that will thrive in its place.

A mixed vignette at Stonecrop Gardens, Cold Spring, New York.

Acknowledgments

From Andrew

It would be difficult to overstate how happy I was to work with Kerry Michaels on this book. I hope her photos inspire you, as they've inspired me. There are never enough words to express my thanks to Brian Katzen, Amanda Thomsen, Pamela Price, Bob, Victoria Harres, Michelle and Michael Forman, Sarah and Jon Guido. Your moral support is incredibly appreciated. Thanks to co-conspirators Kristin Green, Michelle Gervais, Rebecca Sweet, Susan Morrison, Theresa Loe, Angela Treadwell-Palmer, Debra Lee Baldwin, Steve Aitken, and Margaret Roach. Thanks to my friends at Timber Press (and I think I can call you that, after two books).

From Kerry

I first want to thank Andrew Keys for bringing me along on this adventure—it has been a joy. I also want to thank all the amazing people who shared their gardens with me. I am in awe of the passion, artistry, patience, labor, and love it takes to make a truly great garden.

I also want to thank Brett, Ethan, Maya, and my mom, Glenna, for their love and support. Thanks also to my many friends and family members who have shown me so much love, encouragement, and help, and have kept me laughing through this process: Liza Bakewell, Kathy Biberstein, Mary Ann Biberstein, Diane Dreher, Lynn Felici-Gallant, Janet McTeer, Gina Michaels, Brad Michaels, Penny O'Sullivan, and Fiona Wilson to name just a few.

Thanks to Timber Press and to Coastal Maine Botanical Gardens. Thanks to Jack Hyland and Larry Wente, Ellen Lathi, Gordon and Mary Hayward, Andrew Bunting, Maria Nation, James Golden, the owners of the Greenland, New Hampshire, garden, and all the others who so generously shared their magical gardens with me.

PUBLIC GARDENS AND RETAIL NURSERIES

The Arnold Arboretum of Harvard University
Asticou Azalea Garden
Berkshire Botanical Garden
Blithewold Mansion, Gardens, and Arboretum
Broken Arrow Nursery
Chanticleer
Coastal Maine Botanical Gardens
Estabrook's
The Gardens at Elm Bank
Halls Pond Garden
The High Line
Katsura Gardens
Long Hill and Sedgwick Gardens
Longwood Gardens
McLaughlin Garden
New York Botanical Garden
Shakespeare Garden, Central Park
Skillins Greenhouses
Snug Harbor Farm
Stonecrop Gardens
Stonewall Kitchen
Strawbery Banke Museum
Thuya Garden
Tower Hill Botanic Garden

PRIVATE GARDENS AND WHOLESALE NURSERIES

Liza Bakewell
Ball Horticultural Company
Ann Barker
Bedrock Gardens
Andrew Bunting
Mark Brandhorst
Duncan Brine
James Golden
Layne Gregory
Gordon and Mary Hayward
Lynn Heinz
Jack Hyland and Larry Wente
Ellen Lathi
Doug Morris
Maria Nation
Penny O'Sullivan
Owners of the Greenland, New Hampshire, garden
Pleasant View Gardens
Elizabeth Patten
Sakonnet Garden
Joan Benoit Samuelson
Bob Scherer and Jeni Nunnally
P. Allen Smith
Linda Swanson
Van Berkum Nursery

A rill acts as a focal point and an invitation to look further in the garden of Jack Hyland and Larry Wente in Millerton, New York.

Recommended Reading

PART 2: PALETTE

Books

Armitage, Allan M. 2001. *Armitage's Manual of Annuals, Biennials, and Half-Hardy Perennials*. Portland, Oregon: Timber Press.

——.2006. *Armitage's Native Plants for North American Gardens*. Portland, Oregon: Timber Press.

——.2008. *Herbaceous Perennial Plants: A Treatise on Their Identification, Culture and Garden Attributes*. Champaign, Illinois: Stipes Publishing LLC.

——.2010. *Armitage's Vines and Climbers: A Gardener's Guide to the Best Vertical Plants*. Portland, Oregon: Timber Press.

——.2011. *Armitage's Garden Perennials*. 2nd rev. ed. Portland, Oregon: Timber Press.

Benner, Jennifer, and Stephanie Cohen. 2010. *The Nonstop Garden: A Step-by-Step Guide to Smart Plant Choices and Four-Season Designs*. Portland, Oregon: Timber Press.

Brickell, Christopher, and Judith D. Zuk. 1997. *The American Horticultural Society A–Z Encyclopedia of Garden Plants*. New York: DK Publishing.

Burrell, C. Colston. 2006. *Native Alternatives to Invasive Plants*. All-Region Guides, Handbook 185. Brooklyn, New York: Brooklyn Botanic Garden.

Clausen, Ruth Rogers. 2011. *50 Beautiful Deer-Resistant Plants: The Prettiest Annuals, Perennials, Bulbs, and Shrubs that Deer Don't Eat*. Portland, Oregon: Timber Press.

Darke, Rick. 2007. *The Encyclopedia of Grasses for Livable Landscapes*. Portland, Oregon: Timber Press.

Dirr, Michael A. 2011. *Dirr's Encyclopedia of Trees and Shrubs*. Portland, Oregon: Timber Press.

DiSabato-Aust, Tracy. 2009. *50 High-Impact, Low-Care Garden Plants*. Portland, Oregon: Timber Press.

Ellis, Barbara W. 2007. *Covering Ground*. North Adams, Massachusetts: Storey Publishing.

Gerritsen, Henk, and Piet Oudolf. 2011. *Dream Plants for Natural Gardens*. London: Frances Lincoln Limited.

Green, Kristin. 2014. *Plantiful: Start Small, Grow Big with 150 Plants That Spread, Self-Sow, and Overwinter*. Portland, Oregon: Timber Press.

Keys, Andrew. 2012. *Why Grow That When You Can Grow This?: 255 Extraordinary Alternatives to Everyday Problem Plants*. Portland, Oregon: Timber Press.

Ogden, Lauren Springer, and Scott Ogden. 2011. *Waterwise Plants for Sustainable Gardens: 200 Drought-Tolerant Choices for All Climates*. Portland, Oregon: Timber Press.

Ondra, Nancy J. 2007. *Foliage*. North Adams, Massachusetts: Storey Publishing.

Reich, Lee. 2009. *Landscaping with Fruit: Strawberry ground covers, blueberry hedges, grape arbors, and 39 other luscious fruits to make your yard an edible paradise*. North Adams, Massachusetts: Storey Publishing.

Rice, Graham. 2011. *Planting the Dry Shade Garden: The Best Plants for the Toughest Spot in Your Garden*. Portland, Oregon: Timber Press.

Taylor, Jane. 1993. *Drought-Tolerant Plants: Waterwise Gardening for Every Climate*. New York: Prentice Hall.

Websites

Dave's Garden Plantfiles
davesgarden.com/guides/pf

This vertical planting in the garden of Andrew Bunting in Pennsylvania may look complex, but it's held together by foliage, all similar in size.

Fine Gardening Plant Guide
www.finegardening.com/plantguide

Go Botany: New England Wild Flower Society
gobotany.newenglandwild.org

Great Plant Picks
www.greatplantpicks.org

Lady Bird Johnson Wildflower Center Native Plant Database
www.wildflower.org/plants

Missouri Botanical Garden Kemper Center for Home Gardening Plant Finder
www.mobot.org/gardeninghelp/plantfinder

North Carolina State University College of Agriculture and Life Sciences Plant Fact Sheets
www.ces.ncsu.edu/depts/hort/consumer/factsheets/index.html

Plant Information Online–University of Minnesota
plantinfo.umn.edu

Plant Lust
plantlust.com

The Battery Plant Database
www.thebattery.org/plants

University of Connecticut Plant Database
www.hort.uconn.edu/plants/index.html

University of Florida Institute of Food and Agricultural Sciences Southern Trees Fact Sheets
edis.ifas.ufl.edu/department_envhort-trees

PART 3: DESIGN

Books

Cohen, Stephanie, and Nancy J. Ondra. 2005. *The Perennial Gardener's Design Primer*. North Adams, Massachusetts: Storey Publishing.

Culp, David L. 2012. *The Layered Garden: Design Lessons for Year-Round Beauty from Brandywine Cottage*. Portland, Oregon: Timber Press.

Darke, Rick. 2002. *The American Woodland Garden: Capturing the Spirit of the Deciduous Forest*. Portland, Oregon: Timber Press.

Greenlee, John. 2009. *The American Meadow Garden: Creating a Natural Alternative to the Traditional Lawn*. Portland, Oregon: Timber Press.

Hadden, Evelyn J. 2012. *Beautiful No-Mow Yards: 50 Amazing Lawn Alternatives*. Portland, Oregon: Timber Press.

Kingsbury, Noel, and Piet Oudolf. 1999. *Designing with Plants*. Portland, Oregon: Timber Press.

——.2013. *Planting: A New Perspective*. Portland, Oregon: Timber Press.

Ogden, Lauren Springer, and Scott Ogden. 2008. *Plant-Driven Design: Creating Gardens That Honor Plants, Place, and Spirit*. Portland, Oregon: Timber Press.

Penick, Pam. 2013. *Lawn Gone!: Low-Maintenance, Sustainable, Attractive Alternatives for Your Yard*. New York: Ten Speed Press.

PART 4: PRACTICE

Books

Brickell, Christopher, and David Joyce. 2011. *The American Horticultural Society Pruning and Training: The Definitive Guide to Pruning Trees, Shrubs, and Climbers*. New York: DK Publishing.

Deardorff, David, and Kathryn Wadsworth. 2009. *What's Wrong With My Plant? (And How Do I Fix It?): A Visual Guide to Easy Diagnosis and Organic Remedies*. Portland, Oregon: Timber Press.

Del Tredici, Peter, and Stewart T.A. Pickett. 2010. *Wild Urban Plants of the Northeast: A Field Guide*. Ithaca, New York: Comstock Publishing.

DiSabato-Aust, Tracy. 2006. *The Well-Tended Perennial Garden: Planting and Pruning Techniques*. Portland, Oregon: Timber Press.

DiTomaso, Joseph M., Joseph C. Neal, and Richard H. Uva. 1997. *Weeds of the Northeast*. Ithaca, New York: Comstock Publishing.

Hobson, Jake. 2011. *The Art of Creative Pruning: Inventive Ideas for Training and Shaping Trees and Shrubs*. Portland, Oregon: Timber Press.

Lewis, Wayne, and Jeff Lowenfels. 2010. *Teaming with Microbes: The Organic Gardener's Guide to the Soil Food Web*. Portland, Oregon: Timber Press.

Lowenfels, Jeff. 2013. *Teaming with Nutrients: The Organic Gardener's Guide to Optimizing Plant Nutrition*. Portland, Oregon: Timber Press.

Ondra, Nancy J. 2009. *The Perennial Care Manual: A Plant-by-Plant Guide: What to Do & When to Do It*. North Adams, Massachusetts: Storey Publishing.

Reich, Lee. 2010. *The Pruning Book: Completely Revised and Updated*. Newtown, Connecticut: The Taunton Press.

Soderstrom, Neil. 2008. *Deer-Resistant Landscaping: Proven Advice and Strategies for Outwitting Deer and 20 Other Pesky Mammals*. New York: Rodale Books.

Tallamy, Douglas W. 2009. *Bringing Nature Home: How You Can Sustain Wildlife with Native Plants*. Portland, Oregon: Timber Press.

Thomsen, Amanda. 2012. *Kiss My Aster: A Graphic Guide to Creating a Fantastic Yard Totally Tailored to You*. North Adams, Massachusetts: Storey Publishing.

Websites

University of Massachusetts Amherst Soil and Plant Tissue Testing Laboratory
soiltest.umass.edu

University of Connecticut Soil Nutrient Analysis Laboratory
soiltest.uconn.edu

The University of Maine Analytical Laboratory and Maine Soil Testing Service
anlab.umesci.maine.edu

University of New Hampshire Cooperative Extension Soil Testing
extension.unh.edu/Soil-Testing

Cornell University Nutrient Analysis Lab
cnal.cals.cornell.edu

The University of Vermont Agricultural and Environmental Testing Lab
www.uvm.edu/pss/ag_testing

The Pennsylvania State University Agricultural Analytical Services Lab
www.aasl.psu.edu/ssft.htm

Rutgers New Jersey Agricultural Experiment Station Soil Testing Laboratory
njaes.rutgers.edu/soiltestinglab

University of Delaware Soil Testing Program
ag.udel.edu/dstp

University of Rhode Island Soil Testing
www.uri.edu/ce/factsheets/sheets/soiltest.html

Nova Scotia Department of Agriculture Laboratory Services
www.gov.ns.ca/agri/qe/labserv

Prince Edward Island Department of Agriculture and Forestry Soil, Feed, and Water Chemistry Testing Laboratory
www.gov.pe.ca/af/agweb/index.php3?number=74144

A&L Canada Laboratories Inc. Soil Testing
www.alcanada.com/Agricultural-Soil.htm

Mail-Order Sources for Plants

IN THE NORTHEAST

Avant Gardens
Dartmouth, MA
508-998-8819
www.avantgardensne.com

Broken Arrow Nursery
Hamden, CT
203-288-1026
www.brokenarrownursery.com

Fairweather Gardens
Greenwich, NJ
856-451-6261
www.fairweathergardens.com

Fedco Trees
Waterville, ME
207-873-7333
www.fedcoseeds.com/trees.htm

RareFind Nursery
Jackson, NJ
732-833-0613
www.rarefindnursery.com

Tripple Brook Farm
Southampton, MA
413-527-4626
www.tripplebrookfarm.com

Variegated Foliage Nursery
Eastford, CT
860-974-3951
www.variegatedfoliage.com

White Flower Farm
Litchfield, CT
800-503-9624
www.whiteflowerfarm.com

FARTHER AFIELD

United States

Annie's Annuals
Richmond, CA
888-266-4370
www.anniesannuals.com

Antique Rose Emporium
Brenham, TX
800-441-0002
www.antiqueroseemporium.com

Arrowhead Alpines
Fowlerville, MI
517-223-3581
www.arrowhead-alpines.com

Big Dipper Farm
Black Diamond, WA
360-886-8253
www.bigdipperfarm.com

Bluestone Perennials
Madison, OH
800-852-5243
www.bluestoneperennials.com

Brent and Becky's Bulbs
Gloucester, VA
877-661-2852
www.brentandbeckysbulbs.com

Brushwood Nursery
Athens, GA
706-548-1710
www.gardenvines.com

Burnt Ridge Nursery
Onalaska, WA
360-985-2873
www.burntridgenursery.com

Cistus Nursery
Portland, OR
503-621-2233
www.cistus.com

Dancing Oaks Nursery
Monmouth, OR
503-838-6058
www.dancingoaks.com

Digging Dog Nursery
Albion, CA
707-937-1130
www.diggingdog.com

Dove Creek Gardens
Millington, TN
901-829-2306
www.dovecreekgardens.com

Far Reaches Farm
Port Townsend, WA
360-390-5114
www.farreachesfarm.com

Forestfarm
Williams, OR
541-846-7269
www.forestfarm.com

Gardensoyvey
Arlington, TN
888-617-7390
www.gardensoyvey.com

Gossler Farms
Springfield, OR
541-746-3922
www.gosslerfarms.com

High Country Gardens
Santa Fe, NM
800-925-9387
www.highcountrygardens.com

Joy Creek Nursery
Scappoose, OR
503-543-7474
www.joycreek.com

Klehm's Song Sparrow
Avalon, WI
800-553-3715
www.songsparrow.com

Lazy S'S Farm
Barboursville, VA
www.lazyssfarm.com

Mail-Order Natives
Lee, Florida
850-973-6830
www.mailordernatives.com

Nearly Native Nursery
Fayetteville, GA
770-460-6284
www.nearlynativenursery.com

Plant Delights Nursery
Raleigh, NC
919-772-4794
www.plantdelights.com

Prairie Nursery
Westfield, WI
800-476-9453
www.prairienursery.com

Quackin' Grass Nursery
Brooklyn, CT
860-779-1732
www.quackingrassnursery.com

Sunshine Farm and Gardens
Renick, WV
304-497-2208
www.sunfarm.com

Woodlanders
Aiken, SC
803-648-7522
www.woodlanders.net

Canada

Bluestem Nursery
Christina Lake, BC
888-747-6363
www.bluestem.ca

Botanus
Langley, BC
800-672-3413
www.botanus.com

Chuck Chapman Iris
Guelph, ON
519-856-0956
www.chapmaniris.com

Fraser's Thimble Farms
Salt Spring Island, BC
250-537-5788
www.thimblefarms.com

Gardenimport
Richmond Hill, ON
800-339-8314
www.gardenimport.com

Hortico
Waterdown, ON
905-689-6984
www.hortico.com

Wildflower Farm
Coldwater, ON
866-476-9453
www.wildflowerfarm.com

Metric Conversions

INCHES	CENTIMETERS
¼	0.6
½	1.3
¾	1.9
1	2.5
2	5.1
3	7.6
4	10
5	13
6	15
7	18
8	20
9	23
10	25
20	51
30	76
40	100
50	130
60	150
70	180
80	200
90	230
100	250

FEET	METERS
1	0.3
2	0.6
3	0.9
4	1.2
5	1.5
6	1.8
7	2.1
8	2.4
9	2.7
10	3
20	6
30	9
40	12
50	15
60	18
70	21
80	24
90	27
100	30

TEMPERATURES
°C = 5/9 × (°F−32)
°F = (9/5 × °C) + 32

Photography Credits

Kristin Green: 125 top row, right; middle row, center and right; 145 right; 168 third row, right; 171 middle row, left.

Andrew Keys: 36; 37 top left, right; 38 right; 41 right; 42; 43; 44; 45 right; 46 right; 47; 48; 49; 50 bottom; 51 left; 53; 55; 56 right; 58; 59; 60 top; 62 right; 64; 65; 66; 67; 69 top, right; 70 right; 71 right; 73 right; 75; 76; 78; 80 left; 84 left; 85 right; 86; 87; 88 right; 90 top; 92 left; 94; 95 bottom; 97 left; 98 left; 100; 101; 102; 103; 105; 107; 108; 110 left; 111 right; 112; 113 left; 115; 116 left; 119 top; 121 bottom; 124 right; 126 left; 131 left; 132 left; 133; 134; 138; 141; 142; 144 bottom; 148 right; 149 left; 152; 154 left; 156 left; 157; 160 right; 161 left; 165 bottom; 166 right; 170 top row, left; 173; 175 right; 176 right; 177 left; 179; 180; 181 left; 182; 184 right; 186 left; 187 left; 189; 191 right; 193 left; 194 right; 197 right; 206 right; 207; 265; 266; 275.

All other photos by **Kerry Michaels**

Index

About the Authors

PHOTO BY KERRY MICHAELS

PHOTO BY KRISTEN FUNKHOUSER PIERCE

Andrew Keys is a writer, lifelong gardener, and author of *Why Grow That When You Can Grow This?: 255 Extraordinary Alternatives to Everyday Problem Plants* (Timber Press, 2012). Andrew's writing has appeared in *This Old House Magazine* and *Fine Gardening*, and he's produced podcasts for *Fine Gardening* and *Horticulture Magazine*. Andrew has lectured at the Philadelphia Flower Show, Boston Flower Show, Northwest Flower & Garden Show in Seattle, and others. He's trained as an organic land care professional by the Northeast Organic Farming Association.

Kerry Michaels is a photographer, writer, and multimedia producer. Her garden photographs have been seen in many books, magazines, and websites. She is a contributing photographer and writer for *Coastal Home* magazine, and is the writer and photographer for the popular website container-gardening.about.com. Kerry was the co-producer/director of the award-winning documentary film *River of Steel*. Kerry runs Flying Point Photography and lives in Maine with her family.